Intersections:
Where Faith and Life Meet

A Cumberland Presbyterian
Adult Resource
Volume 13, Joy

FAITH
LIFE

Discipleship Ministry Team
Ministry Council
Cumberland Presbyterian Church

8207 Traditional Place
Cordova, Tennessee 38016

First Edition 2016

Published by The Discipleship Ministry Team
General Assembly Ministry Council of the Cumberland Presbyterian Church
Cordova, Tennessee

ISBN-13: 978-0692642191

ISBN-10: 0692642196

We want to hear from you.
Please send your comments about this curriculum to
the Discipleship Ministry Team at chm@cumberland.org

OUR UNITED OUTREACH
Made Possible In Part By Your Tithe To Our United Outreach

Table of Contents

Editor: Cindy Martin
Proofreader: Marsha Hudson

To order, call 901-276-4572, x 252 or e-mail resources@cumberland.org.

Singing for Joy

Scripture for lesson:
Exodus 15:1-21

Written by Marcus Hayes

What simple things bring you joy?

I'm a huge basketball fan. When my favorite team is playing, I am glued to the TV, living and dying with every play. Even though it usually doesn't work, I often try coaching the team from my living room. When there is lackluster and lethargic play, I frequently scream for guys to "play hard" and "dive on the floor." When the team is playing great and things are going well, I can be found on my couch clapping my hands and encouraging the players who, in reality, are hundreds of miles from my home. When a game is close and going down to the wire, I am an absolute mess. There are few things that bring me as much joy as when my team makes a big play or hits the final shot to win the game. Because I am so emotionally invested (trust me, I know it's pathetic!), I become overwhelmed with joy. I jump in the air, scream, and sometimes, I might do a dance. The unrestrained joy of victory is so sweet. And it gives my family something to laugh about!

Prep for the Journey

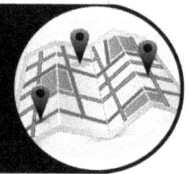

In the Hebrew Bible the title for what we call *Exodus* is literally translated "And these are the names." Exodus tells the story of the people who were led out slavery and into worship. It is a narrative of God taking slaves and making them God's people, a priest to all the nations. The Song of Moses and the Song of Miriam were the immediate expressions of the community's joy for what God had done. So, what exactly is this great thing that God did?

Moses and the Israelites had quite the experience. After the Passover and final plague, in which the Lord struck down all the firstborn in Egypt, Pharaoh finally agreed to let the people go, freeing them from slavery. The people wasted no time, leaving immediately. But like any good emperor, Pharaoh could not just let his labor force leave and get nothing in return. So, he gathered his army and went after the Israelites.

When the Israelites saw Pharaoh's army approaching, they were understandably concerned. As is a common occurrence in Exodus, the people got annoyed with Moses, asking: "Why have you led us out here to die? Were there not enough graves in Egypt? Didn't we tell you just to leave us alone?!"

This community had the debilitating realization that they were so close to freedom, yet so far away as they had come to an impasse at the Red Sea, with Pharaoh's army in hot pursuit. But God would not be outdone. God's beloved people would be freed from their slavery and suffering.

Following God's directions, Moses stretched out his hand over the sea. The sea parted, and the Israelites walked through on dry ground. The Egyptian army didn't have it so easy. Their chariot wheels got stuck in the sand and the waters closed up on them. Israel was safe. God had rescued Israel. God's people were free because of the great work of the Lord.

Within these people was a combination of relief, new life, freedom, and unfettered joy. So what do you do when you have that combination of emotions? You sing, of course!

On the Road

Read Exodus 15:1-3.

Then Moses and the Israelites sang this song to the LORD:

"I will sing to the LORD, for he has triumphed gloriously;
* horse and rider he has thrown into the sea.*
² The LORD is my strength and my might,
* and he has become my salvation;*
this is my God, and I will praise him,
* my father's God, and I will exalt him.*
³ The LORD is a warrior;
* the LORD is his name.*

The first fifteen chapters of Exodus follow a basic plot line: an expressed need, a deep lament by those suffering followed by a word from God and an act of salvation, and then a response of thanksgiving. In fact, you can find this pattern throughout the Old Testament as it is how Israel understood her history with God. The Song of Moses not only participates in the plot line as a response of thanksgiving, but contains it.

The song recounts God's mighty acts in rescuing the Israelites from the pursuits of Pharaoh's army and leading them in the wilderness. Scholars have noted that the Song of Moses is one of the oldest poems and traditions in the Hebrew Scriptures. It articulates Israel's

How do you celebrate joyous occasions? How do you respond when you believe that the joy was brought about by God's active presence in your life?

How do you understand your history with God? How do you think your church views its history with God? Why?

liberation from Egypt, while celebrating God who achieved this act on Israel's behalf.

The first three verses focus on God as the subject of Israel's praise. In these verses Israel was not only offering praise to God, but also declaring that God—and God alone—had acted to liberate them from bondage. Israel would sing with praise and exaltation to God because God had done for Israel what Israel could not have done for herself.

Read Exodus 15:4-10.

"Pharaoh's chariots and his army he cast into the sea;
his picked officers were sunk in the Red Sea.
[5] The floods covered them;
they went down into the depths like a stone.
[6] Your right hand, O LORD, glorious in power—
your right hand, O LORD, shattered the enemy.
[7] In the greatness of your majesty you overthrew your adversaries;
you sent out your fury, it consumed them like stubble.
[8] At the blast of your nostrils the waters piled up,
the floods stood up in a heap;
the deeps congealed in the heart of the sea.
[9] The enemy said, 'I will pursue, I will overtake,
I will divide the spoil, my desire shall have its fill of them.
I will draw my sword, my hand shall destroy them.'
[10] You blew with your wind, the sea covered them;
they sank like lead in the mighty waters.

Verses 4-10 articulate specific acts of might that God performed in liberating Israel: casting Pharaoh's chariots and army into the sea, shattering the enemy, blowing the waters apart, and covering the army that was in hot pursuit. The song recognized Israel's desperate situation and exuberantly proclaimed God's great act in overcoming Israel's oppressors. The song openly declared that the Israelites' rescue was rooted within a historical reality in which God was present and involved. God took action in the historical and political aspects of the people in order to bring freedom to those who were enslaved.

Read Exodus 15:11-19.

"Who is like you, O LORD, among the gods?
Who is like you, majestic in holiness,
awesome in splendor, doing wonders?
[12] You stretched out your right hand,
the earth swallowed them.

[13] "In your steadfast love you led the people whom you redeemed;
you guided them by your strength to your holy abode.
[14] The peoples heard, they trembled;
pangs seized the inhabitants of Philistia.
[15] Then the chiefs of Edom were dismayed;
trembling seized the leaders of Moab;

all the inhabitants of Canaan melted away.
¹⁶ *Terror and dread fell upon them;*
　　by the might of your arm, they became still as a stone
until your people, O LORD, passed by,
　　until the people whom you acquired passed by.
¹⁷ *You brought them in and planted them on the mountain of your own possession,*
　　the place, O LORD, that you made your abode,
　　the sanctuary, O LORD, that your hands have established.
¹⁸ *The LORD will reign forever and ever."*

¹⁹ *When the horses of Pharaoh with his chariots and his chariot drivers went into the sea, the LORD brought back the waters of the sea upon them; but the Israelites walked through the sea on dry ground.*

　　Verses 11-12 are the center of the Song of Moses and are characterized as a doxology, an ascription of praise. The rhetorical question is posed: "Who is like you, O Lord, among the gods?" With a rhetorical question, the answer is already known: no one.

　　Biblical scholar Walter Brueggemann notes that "no other people has a doxology about a god who has won a victory for the oppressed against the oppressor in the real world of power politics" (Brueggemann 800). This act of rescue is placed within a cosmic context in which God overcame chaos and generated an ordered and safe world. God did so because of God's steadfast love for the people. The song leaves no doubt: God redeemed the people and would lead them to the place that God had established for them. Israel was the recipient of this extraordinary and gracious activity. All they could do in response was sing praises.

Read Exodus 15:20-21.
　　Then the prophet Miriam, Aaron's sister, took a tambourine in her hand; and all the women went out after her with tambourines and with dancing. ²¹ And Miriam sang to them:

"Sing to the LORD, for he has triumphed gloriously;
horse and rider he has thrown into the sea."

　　These two verses recollect the song of Miriam, which many believe may be the oldest Hebrew poem. It is believed that the Song of Miriam came first and the Song of Moses is an expansion. However, in its canonical form, the song of Miriam serves as a type of antiphon, reinforcing the thanksgiving that has been sung by the people. This hymn is true to the style of Israel's hymns in its two parts: an imperative summons (Sing to the Lord), and secondly, giving reasons for praise ("For God has done this....")

　　The singing and dancing may have been a liturgical act expressing the joy and exultation for what God had done in liberating and providing well-being. The dancing from the women may have been a dramatic reenactment of the crossing of the Red Sea (Fretheim 162). This liturgical act may have become a standard practice in the

How do you respond to gracious acts? Are you thankful? Do you celebrate? Or do you struggle with grace, thinking that you must repay the person who has gifted you?

How do you respond to liturgical dance? How does it add to or distract from your worship experience?

Moses and the Israelites sang of God's acts and offered praise. Miriam and all the women played the tambourine, danced, and sang. What creative ways might you express praise for the joy that God has brought to your community?

Why go to such great lengths to express gratitude for what God has done? What do you think was behind God's desire for glory? What is behind the human desire for glory?

How does music help you to express joy? sorrow? praise?

In what ways does your church or faith community remember and celebrate God's great acts?

retelling of the Exodus narrative. The drama is celebrated so that Israel may remember their identity as God's people and joyously continue to proclaim God's great acts on their behalf.

Scenic Route

Moses, Miriam, and the rest of the Israelites were not stingy in expressing their overflowing joy for what God had done. Without question, they pulled out all the stops to glorify God: song, dance, and tambourines! This act must be what God desired when he told Moses, "I will gain glory for myself over Pharaoh"

Quite simply, our response to God's activity in the world matters to God. God wanted to gain glory over Pharaoh through the liberation of the Israelites so that the world might know that the God who led with steadfast love was greater than Pharaoh, who oppressed and enslaved. The expression of the joy wrought by God through story, song, dance, and praise was a witness to the whole world of God's goodness. God's reputation was enhanced, and declaring God's mighty acts served as an evangelic proclamation.

Workers Ahead

The act of praising God through song took place over 3,000 years ago and it continues in communities of faith today. Many times people can express their emotions more completely through music than just words.

Identify praise songs or hymns of praise that your church regularly sings in worship. Or use a hymnal to identify such hymns. Join together to read aloud or sing some of these songs. Most of these hymns joyfully proclaim God's cosmic activity, and specifically the salvation that God provided for us in Christ.

Like the ancient Israelites, our realization of salvation and liberation comes to us in the midst of our own personal and historical circumstance. Miriam and all the women praised God for a specific action: "Sing to the LORD…horse and rider he has thrown into the sea." For what do we praise God?

Our praise draws people to God, especially when they hear all that God has done. Talk with others in your group about how your faith community expresses joy and praise to God. Consider ways that you might share this joy over God's activity in the life of your church in such a way that others would be drawn to it.

In the Rear View

Exodus 15 is the byproduct of a community of freed slaves who had exuberant joy in the gracious activity of God. The joy that was generated by God's rescue of them in their dire circumstance resulted in singing, dancing, and shaking the tambourine. The Israelites are a prime example that joy cannot be contained, but must be proclaimed and enthusiastically expressed.

God continues to act in liberating, saving, and gracious ways today. It is important that we express our joy, either in song, dance, or a simple articulation of what God has done for us that we could not have done for ourselves. Such a proclamation gives witness to the world that only God is able to accomplish such things. By offering this proclamation, we are offering an act of worship and expressing our gratitude to God. Expressing our joy is also an act of love, whereby others might hear and see our joy and come to know and experience God's salvation.

How might you and your church express joy for God's goodness? How will this expression impact and minister to your local community?

When has God intervened and acted on behalf of you? your community? your church? How was the joy for God's activity expressed?

What hymn or song of praise do you enjoy singing the most? Share with your group why you find your favorite hymn of praise meaningful.

Travel Log

Day 1:

The songs of Miriam and Moses list specific acts that God had done for the Israelites. While our days may not contain something as grand as the splitting of the Red Sea, take time to consider at least three ways in which God was active with you today. List each instance and offer a prayer of thanksgiving. In your prayer name each of the ways God was active with you.

Day 2:

Read Exodus 15:2. In what ways do you believe that God is your "strength and your might?" Whose strength do you trust more: God's, your own, or someone else's? Think about your reliance upon God and what it would mean to trust in God's strength. Write down your thoughts in the space below.

Day 3:

God liberated the Israelites, but God made use of human agents, most notably, Moses. What person has God used to minister to you and bring you joy? Pray that the Spirit would reveal this "human agent" to you. Write a thank you note to this person, expressing your gratitude for his or her openness to God's work. Jot down some words that will help you remember those things you want to include in your note.

Day 4:

How might you be an agent of liberation for someone? Consider those who are in desperate circumstances and pray for discernment as to how you might participate in bringing them God's liberating joy. Note some ideas below and determine how you can take action on one of them.

Day 5:

Search the Internet for prayers of "Great Thanksgiving" that are used in the liturgy for communion. How do these prayers compare with the Song of Moses? How does offering thanksgiving to God inspire faithfulness? Journal your thoughts.

Day 6:

Write a prayer of thanksgiving, naming either specific or general acts of God for which you want to praise God. Ask your pastor or worship leader if you can offer the prayer during a worship service. In doing so, you will be participating in giving a public proclamation to what God has done.

Day 7:

Search the headlines in a newspaper, online, or those that you hear during a news program. Where do you find instances of God liberating, saving, and bringing joy to people? Who are the "human agents" of God's power in these news stories? How is joy being expressed? Write a sentence or two to describe the story. Give thanks to God for continuing to bring joy to people from all walks of life.

Works Cited:

Brueggemann, Walter. "The Book of Exodus." *The New Interpreter's Bible*. Nashville: Abingdon Press, 1994.

Fretheim, Terence. *Exodus*. Louisville: Westminster John Knox Press, 1991.

Dancing for Joy!

Scripture for lesson:
1 Chronicles 15:11-29

Written by Marcus Hayes

What symbols or objects have meaning to you?

In my office I have a shelf filled with items that some might consider to be junk, but to me they are incredibly significant and sacred. A ceramic depiction of a brick church with a steeple sits behind a glass chalice, with a half-burned candle to one side, and a tattered, old Bible on the other.

The ceramic church was a gift from the family of the first person at whose funeral I officiated. The glass chalice has often been used to hold the "fruit of the vine" in services where I have administered communion. The half-burned candle is taken to church session meetings, where it is lit. As it burns, the flame symbolizes the presence of Christ and the guiding force of the Holy Spirit. The tattered Bible, though no longer used, belonged to my great-grandfather.

When life is hard and struggles abound, I can look to this shelf and remember my calling, my faithful heritage, God's grace, and the generosity of the people with whom I serve. I am also reminded that in life and in death, Christ is present.

Prep for the Journey

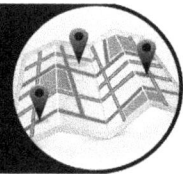

Most people have items of special significance because of their connection to an event or person. For instance, my father's autographed baseball is proudly displayed in his home. My mother has our grandmother's fine china, which she uses only on special occasions. We treasure these objects because they remind us of special people or those things they symbolize.

Ancient Israel's most sacred object was the Ark of the Covenant. The ark was a box, or chest, that was built during the early time of the Israelites' sojourn in the wilderness. Moses placed the tablets on which the Ten Commandments were written in the ark (Deuteronomy 10). Later traditions state that the ark also contained a jar of manna from Israel's wilderness journey, and the rod of Aaron (Hebrews 9:4).

What objects does your church consider to be sacred?

The ark was kept in the tent tabernacle where the people gathered for worship while in the desert. It was designed for mobility, and was fitted with special poles for that purpose. The Levites were designated to carry the ark when it was transported.

Not only did the ark go with the Israelites as they traveled, but in later years they took it into battle with them. The ark's significance was not the physical container, but its representation of the very presence of God and God's covenant relationship with the people.

For over a century, the ark remained at Shiloh. The people built a permanent structure where they could come for worship; the ark was housed in this tabernacle. It was at Shiloh where Hannah prayed for a son and where David went for help when he was hiding from Saul.

On the Road

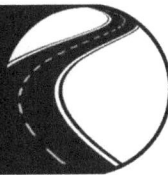

Read 1 Chronicles 15:11-15.

David summoned the priests Zadok and Abiathar, and the Levites Uriel, Asaiah, Joel, Shemaiah, Eliel, and Amminadab. [12] He said to them, "You are the heads of families of the Levites; sanctify yourselves, you and your kindred, so that you may bring up the ark of the Lord, the God of Israel, to the place that I have prepared for it. [13] Because you did not carry it the first time, the Lord our God burst out against us, because we did not give it proper care." [14] So the priests and the Levites sanctified themselves to bring up the ark of the Lord, the God of Israel. [15] And the Levites carried the ark of God on their shoulders with the poles, as Moses had commanded according to the word of the Lord.

This was not David's first attempt at transporting the ark. In chapter 13 David and "the whole assembly of Israel" decided that it was necessary to move the ark out of the city of Kiriath-jearim where it had been for twenty years. According to 1 Samuel 6, the ark was returned to Israel by the Philistines who had captured it, and suffered the consequences (1 Samuel 5). No mention is made of the ark's use or significance during the reign of Saul.

One of David's first acts after being anointed king by all of Israel was to restore the significance of the ark. While Chronicles, unlike Second Samuel, does not narrate the unifying of the tribes of Israel under David, 1 Chronicles 13:1-5 does testify to the unifying of all Israel in response to moving the ark to Jerusalem. However, things did not go smoothly. Uzzah, a driver of the cart, reached out his hand to secure the ark as it was being shaken. In doing so, he touched the ark without being ritually prepared to do so and was struck dead on the spot. David became angry with and afraid of God, and placed the ark in the home of Obed-edom, where it remained for about three months.

What symbols in the church or that are associated with faith have a strong significance to you? Why are they so meaningful?

Why would God strike someone dead who was trying to keep the ark from falling? What does this say about God? What is your reaction to this incident?

What do you do that you consider to be holy and done in service to God? How do you prepare yourself?

How do you feel about the use of instruments other than an organ or piano being used in worship? Why?

How do you see yourself participating in the mission, worship, and ministry of the church? What gifts do you have to offer? How can you use your gifts for God's glory?

After battles with the Philistines, wherein God had "gone out before [David] to strike down the army of the Philistines," David prepared a place for the ark and resumed the ark's transportation to the city of Jerusalem. This time David appointed Levites—the priestly class in ancient Israel—to carry the ark. Unlike Uzzah, the Levites undertook the necessary preparations to sanctify themselves so that they might carry the ark to its resting place in the Holy City.

Read 1 Chronicles 15:16-25.

David also commanded the chiefs of the Levites to appoint their kindred as the singers to play on musical instruments, on harps and lyres and cymbals, to raise loud sounds of joy. ¹⁷ So the Levites appointed Heman son of Joel; and of his kindred Asaph son of Berechiah; and of the sons of Merari, their kindred, Ethan son of Kushaiah; ¹⁸ and with them their kindred of the second order, Zechariah, Jaaziel, Shemiramoth, Jehiel, Unni, Eliab, Benaiah, Maaseiah, Mattithiah, Eliphelehu, and Mikneiah, and the gatekeepers Obed-edom and Jeiel. ¹⁹ The singers Heman, Asaph, and Ethan were to sound bronze cymbals; ²⁰ Zechariah, Aziel, Shemiramoth, Jehiel, Unni, Eliab, Maaseiah, and Benaiah were to play harps according to Alamoth; ²¹ but Mattithiah, Eliphelehu, Mikneiah, Obed-edom, Jeiel, and Azaziah were to lead with lyres according to the Sheminith. ²² Chenaniah, leader of the Levites in music, was to direct the music, for he understood it. ²³ Berechiah and Elkanah were to be gatekeepers for the ark. ²⁴ Shebaniah, Joshaphat, Nethanel, Amasai, Zechariah, Benaiah, and Eliezer, the priests, were to blow the trumpets before the ark of God. Obed-edom and Jehiah also were to be gatekeepers for the ark.

²⁵ So David and the elders of Israel, and the commanders of the thousands, went to bring up the ark of the covenant of the LORD from the house of Obed-edom with rejoicing.

The Levites appointed those who would be musicians and gatekeepers as the ark was paraded into Jerusalem. (Kudos if you attempted to read every name aloud!) The singers were divided into groups of those who would play cymbals, harps, and lyres. The ark represented the very presence of God, and symbolized God's covenant relationship with the people. The people of Israel believed that when the ark was present, God was present, which called for a joyous celebration.

It is unique that the chronicler not only names David and the priests, but also the musicians who participated in the ark's transportation. By including their names, he affirmed that anyone who takes part in the holy work of God matters and is valued.

Read 1 Chronicles 15:25-28.

So David and the elders of Israel, and the commanders of the thousands, went to bring up the ark of the covenant of the LORD from the house of Obed-edom with rejoicing. ²⁶ And because God helped the Levites who were carrying the ark of the covenant of the LORD, they sacrificed seven bulls and seven rams. ²⁷ David was clothed with a robe of fine linen, as also were all the Levites who were carrying the ark, and the singers, and Chenaniah the leader of the music of the singers; and David wore a linen ephod. ²⁸ So all Israel brought up the ark of the covenant of the LORD with shouting, to the sound of the horn, trumpets, and cymbals, and made loud music on harps and lyres.

Leading the grand parade down Main Street in Jerusalem were David, the elders of Israel, and the Levites as they carried the ark for all to see. Think of a marching band leading a local holiday parade with the mayor and town leaders dancing and shouting as they make their way through the city. What a sight! The ark—the symbolic object of God's presence—had arrived. In other words, the people of Jerusalem and all Israel had a visual affirmation that God was present in their city and was abiding with them. Hallelujah!

The presence of the ark in Jerusalem had religious and political implications. David had great concern for proper worship, the priesthood, and music. By bringing the ark to his capital, he was establishing Jerusalem as the Holy City. Solomon would eventually build the Temple in Jerusalem, symbolizing the joining of heaven (God's realm) with earth (humanity's realm). As Christians we affirm this symbolic joining in the person of Jesus of Nazareth, who is the word of God made flesh, and in the ministry of the Holy Spirit.

Having the ark in Jerusalem was also a politically-motivated act designed to unite the tribes of Israel into one nation. The Ark of the Covenant was an important symbol for all of Israel. By bringing it into and celebrating its presence in Jerusalem, David established Jerusalem as the political and religious center of the kingdom. The celebration and the ark's procession was a unifying act that brought harmony to the people of God.

Scenic Route

49 MILE
SCENIC ROUTE
←

When interpreting a biblical text it is interesting not only to explore the history of the time to which the text refers, but also to consider the history of when the text was written. It is likely that the author of Chronicles was writing for a specific group of people who were dealing with their own struggle of faithfulness amidst their historical circumstances. It can be fruitful to consider not only what the scripture says, but to what it is responding and the message that is being communicated via narrative.

Chronicles is one of the later writings in the Old Testament. It was likely written after Judah and Jerusalem had fallen to Babylon. During this time the Temple was destroyed, the Davidic monarchy

What joyous times might entire communities celebrate? What form might these celebrations take?

In what ways are people of faith divided today? Under what symbols or affirmations might we find unity? Why is such unity important?

Where do you find hope in tragedy? How does your hope manifest itself?

Have you ever been angry at or afraid of God? Why? How do you believe God responds to those who are angry at God?

Consider times when you were angry at God. How free did you feel to express your anger?

was dethroned, and the people were exiled. Eventually, under the rule of Cyrus the Persian, the exiles were allowed to return to Jerusalem. They found a destroyed city, a demolished Temple, and foreign rule.

Chronicles attempts to reinterpret Israel's history in light of her tragic context (Harris and Platzner). The returned exiles worked to rebuild the Temple and establish it as a holy place where God would continue to dwell, even though there was not a king on David's throne, which God had promised (2 Samuel 7:13). For the chronicler, all had been stripped away except for the clinging hope that even in tragedy God was still present with God's people. In telling of the joyous procession that brought the ark into Jerusalem, the chronicler was affirming and celebrating that God still dwelt with the covenant community. God had not abandoned them and God will not abandon us. Let us make music and dance with joy!

Workers Ahead

After David's first failed attempt to bring the ark to Jerusalem, the chronicler noted that David was angry with and afraid of God that day. Why wouldn't he have been? He was trying to do the right thing, and so was Uzzah, but Uzzah ended up dead. Uzzah was not ritually cleared to touch the ark—but couldn't God have forgiven that of someone who was trying to keep the ark from falling? While the presence of God can be a blessing (1 Chronicles 13:14), and God is "merciful and gracious, slow to anger" (Exodus 34:6), the presence of God can sometimes be dangerous.

That being said, God did not hold David's anger and grief against him. David placed the ark in the home of Obed-edom, and God blessed Obed-edom's home. God gave David time and space to work up the courage to resume his task. God even remained active in David's life and pursuits (1 Chronicles 14:15). Our anger is not too much for God to handle. It is almost as if God understood David's frustration. Because God remained faithful to David, David remained faithful to God. The ark was brought into Jerusalem and anger and fear gave way to rejoicing and dancing. God will remain faithful to us, even in our anger.

In the Rear View

David's efforts to bring the ark to Jerusalem brought about singing and dancing as the ark was paraded through the city. This demonstration of pageantry and its retelling serves a couple of purposes. The celebration of the ark, and its return to the religious center of the covenant community, united a divided people in their common faith. It was also a symbolic representation of the presence of God. No matter what happened, the faithful would know that God had not abandoned them. The manifestation and sacredness of God's presence is enough to bring joy out of anger and despair.

In what situations do we need to work for unity today? How might that work take place?

Travel Log

Day 1:

Most faithful persons experience times when they are afraid of God (or of God's consequences), or angry at God. When have you experienced such a time? How was God's grace and presence amidst your anger made known to you? Read Psalm 30 and write about your experience.

Day 2:

The Ark of the Covenant symbolized God's presence with the people. What are some sacred symbols for you and your faith community? What do they mean and represent in your life of faith? Jot them down, or draw a picture of these meaningful symbols.

Day 3:

The writer of Chronicles listed the names of those who took part in the sacred act of transporting the ark to Jerusalem. In your church, who actively participates in the church's ministry but goes unnoticed? Are they musicians, custodians, etc.? Jot down their names and write each one a thank you note expressing your gratitude for what they do, or consider publicly acknowledging their service at a church gathering.

Day 4:

In what ways do you serve your church? What acts do you perform, or what roles do you fill that are part of the church's ministry? Make a list of these acts and roles. Then think about other ways you might contribute to the ministry of your church. List those ways also. Evaluate how you can use your gifts.

Day 5:

Many faithful people experience what feels like God's absence. Have you experienced such a time? Was there anything that helped you to know you were not alone? Read Psalm 44:17-26 and write about your experience.

Day 6:

First Chronicles 15:25-28 narrates a joyous celebration of a new time. Does your church have a story that parallels this one? If you have trouble identifying an instance, consider interviewing a long-time member in your congregation to discover times when God's presence was joyously celebrated. Record the events in the space below.

Day 7:

After exploring the stories of your church, consider your own narrative. Do you have a story or experience that recalls the joyous presence of God in your life? Briefly write it down. How does remembering this story encourage you and give you hope?

Works Cited:

Birch, Bruce C. "Ark of the Covenant." Doob Sakenfield, Katherine, et al. *The New Interpreters Dictionary of the Bible: Volume 1*. Nashville: Abingdon Press, 2006. 263-269.

Harris, Stephen L. and Robert L. Platzner. *The Old Testament: An Introduction to the Hebrew Bible*. Boston: McGraw-Hill, 2003.

The Roller Coaster of Faith

Scripture for lesson:
Psalms 122; 86; 51; 32

Written by Marcus Hayes

My wife loves roller coasters. I like roller coasters, too, but we never enjoy them together. Though the thrills—the ups and downs, the curves to the right and to the left, the speed and sudden stops—can be exciting, I usually end up losing my lunch. I am highly susceptible to motion sickness, which causes me to vomit and then leaves me feeling uneasy for the rest of the day. After riding a roller coaster, my one desire is to go directly to a bench, lie down, and not move for at least an hour. As you might imagine, I'm not the most fun person with whom to ride roller coasters! And yet, even though they leave me nauseated afterwards, I do enjoy the thrill and excitement of riding them. Even though there are ups and downs (literally), excitement and sickness, the ride makes it (almost) worthwhile.

Prep for the Journey

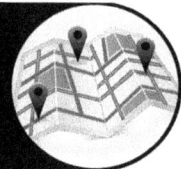

A common metaphor used to describe spirituality and a relationship with God is that of a journey or pilgrimage. However, due to constant change and life's unpredictability, a roller coaster ride might also serve as an adequate description of the life of faith. A relationship with God that is lived in this world goes through many ups and downs, victories and defeats, struggles and celebrations. Such is life.

The Book of Psalms contains Israel's prayers, songs, and poetry. The psalms give expression to a life lived with God in the muck and mire of our broken world. They reflect a range of emotions and experiences, ranging from praise-filled worship to cries of help and laments. Particularly, those psalms associated with David give insight into a relationship with God from one who is "after God's own heart." While these psalms may be reflective of David's relationship with God, they also articulate a spirituality of anyone who would be involved with God.

What metaphors might you use to describe a life of faith?

24

By exploring the psalms of David, we may gain insight into our own relationship with God. Though the roller coaster of faith may lead us to joy, authentic faith will take us there through brokenness, struggles with sin, and pain. Through it all we learn that we are loved and we trust that God will do for us what we could not do for ourselves. Hop on for the ride as we explore Psalms 122; 86; 51; and 32. Though not in numerical order, the order is reflective of the ups and downs that one experiences in a life of faith.

On the Road

Read Psalm 122.

I was glad when they said to me,
"Let us go to the house of the LORD!"
² Our feet are standing
within your gates, O Jerusalem.

³ Jerusalem—built as a city
that is bound firmly together.
⁴ To it the tribes go up,
the tribes of the LORD,
as was decreed for Israel,
to give thanks to the name of the LORD.
⁵ For there the thrones for judgment were set up,
the thrones of the house of David.

⁶ Pray for the peace of Jerusalem:
"May they prosper who love you.
⁷ Peace be within your walls,
and security within your towers."
⁸ For the sake of my relatives and friends
I will say, "Peace be within you."
⁹ For the sake of the house of the LORD our God,
I will seek your good.

Psalm 122 is part of a collection of psalms that are each identified as a "Song of Ascents." It is believed that these psalms were originally used by travelers who were on a pilgrimage to Jerusalem to celebrate a religious festival. Jerusalem was the Holy City of David and the capital of Judea. More importantly, the Temple was located in Jerusalem. The Temple was the religious center of ancient Israel, which is where the people went to offer sacrifices to God. The people of Israel also believed that the Temple was God's dwelling place, the holy space where the presence and glory of God resided with the people.

What ups and downs have you experienced in your faith journey? How have they strengthened your faith?

Where do you go when you are seeking God? Why?

25

When has your faith brought you excitement? How has a desire to be in the presence of God motivated you?

How does your relationship with God inspire you to seek what is good for others?

The excitement of the pilgrim is palpable in verse one. The psalm begins and ends by referring to the "house of the Lord," emphasizing that ascending to Jerusalem was not only the destination, but also the motivation for the pilgrim. He or she desires to be near to and in the presence of God.

Though the pilgrim might have been experiencing conflict and struggle, Jerusalem was viewed as a place of peace and prosperity (verses 6-7) because God's dwelling place was there. The pilgrim undertook the journey hoping for peace and well-being, not only for the self, but for others as well. The journey into God's presence seems to have initiated a transformation that enabled the pilgrim to seek peace for friends, family (verse 8), and that which was good for the "house of the LORD our God." Thus, an individual's journey of faith not only concerns the self, but cares for and takes place within a broader community.

Read Psalm 86.

Incline your ear, O LORD, and answer me,
for I am poor and needy.
² Preserve my life, for I am devoted to you;
save your servant who trusts in you.
You are my God; ³ be gracious to me, O Lord,
for to you do I cry all day long.
⁴ Gladden the soul of your servant,
for to you, O Lord, I lift up my soul.
⁵ For you, O Lord, are good and forgiving,
abounding in steadfast love to all who call on you.
⁶ Give ear, O LORD, to my prayer;
listen to my cry of supplication.
⁷ In the day of my trouble I call on you,
for you will answer me.

⁸ There is none like you among the gods, O Lord,
nor are there any works like yours.
⁹ All the nations you have made shall come
and bow down before you, O Lord,
and shall glorify your name.
¹⁰ For you are great and do wondrous things;
you alone are God.
¹¹ Teach me your way, O LORD,
that I may walk in your truth;
give me an undivided heart to revere your name.
¹² I give thanks to you, O Lord my God, with my whole heart,
and I will glorify your name forever.
¹³ For great is your steadfast love toward me;
you have delivered my soul from the depths of Sheol.

¹⁴ O God, the insolent rise up against me;
a band of ruffians seeks my life,

and they do not set you before them.
15 But you, O Lord, are a God merciful and gracious,
   slow to anger and abounding in steadfast love and faithfulness.
16 Turn to me and be gracious to me;
   give your strength to your servant;
   save the child of your serving girl.
17 Show me a sign of your favor,
   so that those who hate me may see it and be put to shame,
   because you, LORD, have helped me and comforted me.

While Psalm 122 articulates the excitement of faith, Psalm 86 expresses a longing for God's help in times of need and conflict. The psalmist begins by pleading that God hear and answer his petitions because he is in a desperate condition. Though we don't know the exact situation, the psalmist is identified as poor and needy (verse 1), in trouble (verse 7), threatened by a "band of ruffians" (verse 14), and hated (verse 17). I think it's safe to assume the psalmist was having a bad day!

However, though the psalm might be motivated by the psalmist's bad day, the focus of the psalm is an appeal to God and God's character. The psalmist cries out for God's mercy and preservation, and does so trusting that God will hear the cry and is capable of helping. Verses 1-7 identify God as merciful, good, forgiving, loving, and sovereign. These words of identification continue in verses 8-13 where the psalmist made grand proclamations about the incomparability of God. Not only is God sovereign and unrivaled, God expresses "steadfast love" toward the faithful and has performed acts of salvation (verse 13). God is capable of helping in a time of need, and God can be trusted because of God's mercy, grace, steadfast love, and faithfulness (verse 15). God's love is so great that it can be trusted even during dark or difficult times. Because of such great love and fidelity, the psalmist desired to respond faithfully by giving thanks to God and glorifying God's name forever (verse12).

Read Psalm 51.
Have mercy on me, O God,
   according to your steadfast love;
according to your abundant mercy
   blot out my transgressions.
2 Wash me thoroughly from my iniquity,
   and cleanse me from my sin.

3 For I know my transgressions,
   and my sin is ever before me.
4 Against you, you alone, have I sinned,
   and done what is evil in your sight,
so that you are justified in your sentence
   and blameless when you pass judgment.
5 Indeed, I was born guilty,
   a sinner when my mother conceived me.

When have you sought God's help or intervention in your life? Did you feel like God responded? Why or why not?

What words would you use to describe your experience with God/God's character? How has this discovery of who God is impacted your faithfulness?

⁶ *You desire truth in the inward being;*
therefore teach me wisdom in my secret heart.
⁷ *Purge me with hyssop, and I shall be clean;*
wash me, and I shall be whiter than snow.
⁸ *Let me hear joy and gladness;*
let the bones that you have crushed rejoice.
⁹ *Hide your face from my sins,*
and blot out all my iniquities.

¹⁰ *Create in me a clean heart, O God,*
and put a new and right spirit within me.
¹¹ *Do not cast me away from your presence,*
and do not take your holy spirit from me.
¹² *Restore to me the joy of your salvation,*
and sustain in me a willing spirit.

¹³ *Then I will teach transgressors your ways,*
and sinners will return to you.
¹⁴ *Deliver me from bloodshed, O God,*
O God of my salvation,
and my tongue will sing aloud of your deliverance.

¹⁵ *O Lord, open my lips,*
and my mouth will declare your praise.
¹⁶ *For you have no delight in sacrifice;*
if I were to give a burnt offering, you would not be pleased.
¹⁷ *The sacrifice acceptable to God is a broken spirit;*
a broken and contrite heart, O God, you will not despise.

¹⁸ *Do good to Zion in your good pleasure;*
rebuild the walls of Jerusalem,
¹⁹ *then you will delight in right sacrifices,*
in burnt offerings and whole burnt offerings;
then bulls will be offered on your altar.

Psalm 51 articulates and expresses another twist in a life lived with God. Though similar to Psalm 86 in its tone and plea for God's help, the struggle in Psalm 51 is more inward as it involves the psalmist's sinfulness. The words included above this psalm connect it to Nathan's confrontation with David after David sinned by committing adultery with Bathsheba. In an attempted cover-up, David had Bathsheba's husband, Uriah, killed in battle (2 Samuel 11–12). Although the context of this psalm was for a specific incident, it speaks to all those who struggle with the guilt of their own sinfulness. Psalm 51 is as much about God's character and response to sin as it is about human sinfulness.

Before the psalmist makes mention of "sin" or "transgression," in verse 1 there is an appeal to God's character based on who the psalmist believes God to be. God is one who has mercy, steadfast love, and compassion (NIV). Therefore, the psalmist is confident in asking God

How do you think God reacts to your sins? How might this psalm help you as you struggle with your own sinfulness?

to "blot out my transgressions." Verses 3-5 convey the inevitability of human sin and brokenness. Sin is a condition that affects us all, despite our best intentions. However, verses 6-17 propose that sin does not hold the final word about humanity. God's steadfast love, mercy, and compassion are a greater reality than that of our sin. The psalmist would readily proclaim that God's grace is "greater than all our sin."

The psalmist is clear that this forgiveness and mercy is not "cheap grace." By God's action, a person will be given a "clean heart" and a "new and right spirit" (verse 10). The scriptures continually testify to God's ability and willingness to rehabilitate and re-create sinners. David's story is our story.

The "new creation" vows in verse 13 to share the experience of grace and newness with other "transgressors." The one who has been reconciled will testify to reconciliation. God calls and uses those who have sinned to participate in God's reconciling ministry. God's ministry to the world through the church is carried out by sinners. The joy of salvation is that God remakes us and counts us as worthy to carry out this holy vocation.

Read Psalm 32.

Happy are those whose transgression is forgiven,
whose sin is covered.
2 Happy are those to whom the LORD imputes no iniquity,
and in whose spirit there is no deceit.

3 While I kept silence, my body wasted away
through my groaning all day long.
4 For day and night your hand was heavy upon me;
my strength was dried up as by the heat of summer. Selah

5 Then I acknowledged my sin to you,
and I did not hide my iniquity;
I said, "I will confess my transgressions to the LORD,"
and you forgave the guilt of my sin. Selah

6 Therefore let all who are faithful
offer prayer to you;
at a time of distress, the rush of mighty waters
shall not reach them.
7 You are a hiding place for me;
you preserve me from trouble;
you surround me with glad cries of deliverance. Selah

8 I will instruct you and teach you the way you should go;
I will counsel you with my eye upon you.
9 Do not be like a horse or a mule, without understanding,
whose temper must be curbed with bit and bridle,
else it will not stay near you.

In what ways have you experienced God's forgiveness? How difficult is it to believe that God forgives all of your sins?

How has God used you in spite of your past or weaknesses? How have you seen God use others?

In your experience, how has forgiveness—either from God or people—impacted a relationship?

In what ways does a relationship with God bring you joy? How do you let others see that joy?

How difficult is it to see yourself as God's "beloved?" Why might it be easier to believe this about someone else than about yourself?

[10] Many are the torments of the wicked,
    but steadfast love surrounds those who trust in the LORD.
[11] Be glad in the LORD and rejoice, O righteous,
    and shout for joy, all you upright in heart.

In Psalm 32, the roller coaster of faith swings upward, as we are provided with a natural transition from Psalm 51. Psalm 32 is typically labeled as a psalm of thanksgiving as it articulates the joy and gratitude of one who has confessed and been delivered from sin by God's graciousness. The excitement of the psalm is expressed in the opening line: "Happy are those whose transgression is forgiven." Verses 1-2 define happiness and joy in terms of God's forgiveness. To be in a right relationship with God is not a matter of being sinless. Rather, it about being forgiven of sin and trusting in God. Though sin and its effects are often unavoidable, the faithful have the joyous opportunity of seeking God's forgiveness and guidance, which leads to restoration, preservation, and joy.

Verse 5 signals a transition in the psalm. The psalmist acknowledges and confesses his sin, and announces God's forgiveness. After this proclamation, none of the words for sin occur again in the psalm. After forgiveness, the psalmist is able to move forward, growing in faithfulness and rejoicing in what God has done.

Scenic Route

These psalms of David reiterate that faith is a journey of discovering who we are and who God is. On our darkest days, we are people searching for purpose, dealing with conflict, overcome with trouble, overwhelmed by guilt, and broken by sin. Yet God is merciful, compassionate, gracious, abounding in steadfast love, reliable, and capable of renewing our lives. A life of faith lived with God transforms how we see ourselves and our place in the world. We discover that we are forgiven, beloved, and set apart for holy and purposeful living. By seeing ourselves as God sees us, we can be restored to joy, a joy that is infectious as we walk along with others in this sacred pilgrimage.

Workers Ahead

Psalm 32:6 and Psalm 86:2 acknowledge the role of the "faithful," or the "devoted." Both of these words are translated from the Hebrew word *hasid*. This word is derived from the Hebrew word *hesed*, which is commonly translated as "steadfast love." This steadfast love "surrounds those who trust in the LORD" in Psalm 32:10. Thus, it should be noted that those who are faithful to God gain their identity not from their own accomplishment, but from God's loving and gracious act in forgiving and renewing them. God's love and forgiveness is not only the source of our identity, but also what generates our happiness and joy.

In the Rear View

These psalms give witness to the roller coaster that is a life lived in relationship with God. From excitement to despair, and guilt to renewal, such a life is filled with enough ups, downs, and curves to leave us feeling overwhelmed. However, the one constant is God. Though life may be filled with a range of emotions and experiences, through it all God remains gracious, loving, and faithful to those who place their faith in God.

What does it mean to see yourselves as a people who are brought together and formed by God's love? How might your group, or your church, let individuals know that they are loved, forgiven, and claimed as God's? How can you best express God's willingness to act in a person's life to someone?

Travel Log

Day 1:

The four psalms reflect a range of emotions: excitement, despair, guilt, happiness, and joy as well as the ups and downs of life and faith. Reflect upon times in your life when you were filled with joy and times when you were filled with despair. Make a chart of those experiences, and journal about God's role and presence during each circumstance.

Day 2:

Psalms 51 and 32 discuss the necessity of confessing one's sin. Jot down some specific sins with which you struggle. Pray for God's forgiveness, specifically praying Psalm 51:10-12.

Day 3:

The psalms call upon God because of whom the psalmist believed God to be. Read Psalm 86:15-16. Reflect upon your own life of faith. Note three attributes or characteristics of God that articulate your experience of God.

Day 4:

Look back at what you did on days one through three. Write a prayer of thanksgiving to God for what God has done in your life. (For guidance re-read Psalm 32.)

Day 5:

A life of faith in God is not merely inward focused, but also seeks the well-being of others (Psalm 122:8-9). In what ways might you be an agent of God's steadfast love for someone else? Consider how you might show a specific act of love to someone this day, or volunteer your time with a ministry or organization that assists people in need. Journal your thoughts as you consider where you can best show love and how you will do so.

Day 6:

Psalm 86 is written from the perspective of someone who is poor and needy and in a "day of trouble." Read through a news source and pay attention to stories of individuals or communities that could be identified as poor and needy. Make a list of these individuals and/or communities.

Read Psalm 86:13-17 and pray that this individual/community would experience God's deliverance. Consider how you can participate in God's deliverance.

Day 7:

Read Psalm 32:11 throughout your day. Write it down and carry it with you. Simply give thanks to God. Choose to be glad. Rejoice. Express your joy wherever you may be. Write down those things for which you are giving thanks, those things that bring you joy.

Music Brings Joy

Scripture for lesson:
1 Chronicles 16:28-38

Written by Marcus Hayes

I have a group of close friends, yet we all live hours apart. We don't get to see one another as much as we would like, but when we do get together, we make the most of it. A lot of our time together is spent fellowshipping and conversing about life, work, and everything else. It's usually mundane until someone pulls out a guitar and starts playing hit songs from the 90s. We put all our conversations on pause and begin to sing along—even those of us who aren't gifted singers, to say the least. We feel no shame.

The singing serves to harmonize our group and bond us even more closely. No matter what the song is, the simple act of putting words to music has the ability to bring us unity and joy.

Prep for the Journey

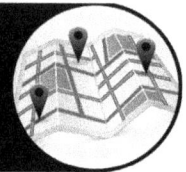

Nothing stirs us or gets our attention like a good song. Music is a big part of everyone's life, even if we are not musicians! Whenever there is a large public event, it usually begins by honoring the country through the singing of the national anthem. When our favorite songs come on the radio, we can't help it—we have to turn up the volume and sing along. Music is not only enjoyable, but like poetry, it communicates our deepest emotions and truths that are difficult to render in any other form of communication.

The covenant community has long known the importance of music. Faith is not only confessed with verbal affirmation and right practice, it is sung. When we gather, we express our faith through songs and hymns. Ancient Israel followed this practice using psalms that express myriad emotions: praise, thanksgiving, joy, lament, and cries for help. Singing was a way in which the faithful entered into the presence of God and nurtured their relationship with God.

In 1 Chronicles 16 David brought the Ark of the Covenant to Jerusalem. The ark was paraded into town with shouting, music, and

What types of music or songs do you find meaningful? Why are they special to you?

How does music help you to feel closer to God?

36

dancing. Finally, the ark—the symbolic indicator of God's presence with the people—rested in the capital city. David pitched a tent to serve as the dwelling place of the ark until the Temple was built.

In acknowledgment of the holiness of the ark, David appointed Levites to perform specific tasks that would assure the ark received proper care. The Levites were charged with invoking, thanking, and praising the Lord before the Ark of the Covenant. A Levite named Asaph was appointed as the leader of those who would offer praises to the Lord through song.

On the Road

Read 1 Chronicles 16:28-33.

Ascribe to the Lord, O families of the peoples,
*   ascribe to the Lord glory and strength.*
29 Ascribe to the Lord the glory due his name;
*   bring an offering, and come before him.*
Worship the Lord in holy splendor;
*   30 tremble before him, all the earth.*
*   The world is firmly established; it shall never be moved.*
31 Let the heavens be glad, and let the earth rejoice,
*   and let them say among the nations, "The Lord is king!"*
32 Let the sea roar, and all that fills it;
*   let the field exult, and everything in it.*
33 Then shall the trees of the forest sing for joy
*   before the Lord, for he comes to judge the earth.*

The singing of praises begins in verse 8 of chapter 16 and continues through verse 36. These verses are the combination of parts of three psalms of praise and are slightly adapted from Psalm 96:7-13.

Though the Israelites sang these praises, the theological thrust is that the praise of God was not limited to the covenant community of Israel. Verse 28 begins with "Ascribe to the Lord, O families of the peoples, ascribe to the Lord glory and strength." Even though Israel was singing before the ark, they recognized that praise must arise from all people of the earth. Israel had a role to play in bringing forth that praise.

When God called Abraham to leave his father's house so that God could make of him a great nation, God told Abraham, "I will bless those who bless you, and the one who curses you I will curse; and in you all the families of the earth shall be blessed" (Genesis 12:3). Israel's role as a chosen people was not to be self-serving. Rather, as they were blessed by God, they must bless others, so that all families of the earth could join in singing praise to God.

How can you share God's blessings so that others might give praise to God? How do faith communities different from your own offer praise to God? What is similar? different?

What role does nature play in your faith life? As Christians, what is our responsibility to the earth and its well-being? How do you think the natural world praises God?

Verses 30-33 expand the notion that Israel was not the sole entity capable of praising God. This part of the psalm expands the praise of God beyond humanity and into the natural world. The heavens and the earth will join the nations in proclaiming "The LORD is king!" The sea and all that is in it roars, the fields and all in them exult, and the trees sing for joy. What a sight to behold!

This psalm is intent on communicating that God is in a relationship of care and faithfulness with the natural world and that nature responds with praise because God has generated stability and calmed the world's chaos (16:30). Bible Scholar J. Clinton McCann comments that "The destiny of humankind and the destiny of the earth are inseparable. We—people, plants, and even inanimate entities—are all in this together" (1066). We—humanity and the natural world—are all creations of a loving and faithful God. We can't help but join together in harmony to produce praise for our Creator.

Read 1 Chronicles 16:34-36.
³⁴ *O give thanks to the LORD, for he is good;*
  for his steadfast love endures forever.

³⁵ *Say also:*

"Save us, O God of our salvation,
  and gather and rescue us from among the nations,
that we may give thanks to your holy name,
  and glory in your praise.
³⁶ *Blessed be the LORD, the God of Israel,*
  from everlasting to everlasting."

Then all the people said "Amen!" and praised the LORD.

This part of the song is derived from Psalm 106:1, 47-48. Verse 34 is a common refrain within Chronicles and the psalms. Israel was given the imperative: "Give thanks to the LORD." Why? The psalm answers: "for [God] is good." How do we know that God is good? Again, the psalm answers itself: "for [God's] steadfast love endures forever."

In what ways do you experience God's unending love? How is it communicated to you? How do you share this love with others?

The phrase *steadfast love* could also be translated as *covenant loyalty* or *faithfulness*. It is meant to communicate God's special relationship with God's people, a relationship of love that is faithful, loyal, and persistent. As the psalmist notes, God's steadfast love is not temporary, nor will it be withdrawn. It endures forever.

Verse 35 offers a plea for God to save the people of Israel so that they might continue to give praise. Such an appeal arises from Israel's perceived identity. Biblical scholar Ellen Davis observes that Israel knew itself as a people who had been preserved and kept in faith against incredible odds for the express purpose of praising God. Their praise of God was a central characteristic of who they believed themselves to be. Thus, when they found themselves in trouble, they pleaded for God's salvation so that they might continue to praise God: "Save us... gather us and rescue us... that we may give thanks to your

38

holy name." Verse 36 concludes the song of praise by blessing God. The text notes that after the "amen!" the people continued in their praise.

Read 1 Chronicles 16:37-38.

David left Asaph and his kinsfolk there before the ark of the covenant of the LORD to minister regularly before the ark as each day required, ³⁸ and also Obed-edom and his sixty-eight kinsfolk; while Obed-edom son of Jeduthun and Hosah were to be gatekeepers.

These two verses note those whom David selected to oversee the praise and adoration that would be done before the ark. Asaph and his family were to "minster regularly before the ark." Asaph was the Levite who had served as the chief musician when the ark was brought into Jerusalem (16:5). It is also believed that he founded a school of singers called the "sons of Asaph," to whom many of the psalms are attributed.

Obed-edom was appointed to be the gatekeeper. He had faithfully stored the Ark of the Covenant in his home after David and the Israelites failed to sanctify themselves properly before attempting to transport the ark (1 Chronicles 13). Though David was the king—serving as the political and religious leader of the people—the ministry of praise and adoration of God was shared amongst other faithful and gifted persons.

Scenic Route

Within the narrative context of First Chronicles, these psalms were sung during a time of perceived accomplishment and peace. David had defeated the Philistines, established Jerusalem as the capital city, united the kingdom, and brought the Ark of the Covenant to dwell in Jerusalem. It appeared as though God had shown favor on David and the nation of Israel. Everything was great and they were aware of God's goodness! So why wouldn't they offer praise?!

Chronicles was one of the later writings in the Old Testament, likely coming sometime after the exiles had been able to return home from Babylon. Though the exile had ended, Israel and Judah remained under foreign rule, lacking independence. By including the section of the psalm that sings "Save us, O God… gather and rescue us from among the nations…" the chronicler may have been influenced by the lack of independence and the political pressure of his day.

It should be noted that psalms of praise, and praise of God in general, are not isolated from the difficulties of human life. Rather, praise of God is sung in response to and with a full awareness of life's trag-

How can or do you offer praise to God outside of communal worship? What would be most likely to cause you to burst into a song of praise?

In what ways might you contribute to the organization and leading of your church's communal worship?

How does the historical context of this passage affect your understanding of it?

How does your faith guide you through difficult times? How easy is it for you to praise God in difficult circumstances?

Do we, as humans, often become self-centered in how we envision God's love and care? As a result, do we exploit the natural world instead of affirming its goodness?

edies and struggles. Giving praise to God allows us to see the world as God does: holy and within the sphere of God's care. No matter what may come our way, we maintain that our faith is in the one who firmly established the earth (16:30). In spite of all forces that seek to control us, we continually proclaim "the Lord is king" (16:31), and we continue in our faith because God "is good; for his steadfast love endures forever." (16:34)

Workers Ahead

The psalmist made sure to include all aspects of the natural world, calling them to rejoice and worship the Lord. The heavens, the earth, the sea (and all that fills it), the field (and everything in it), the trees and forest joined the people in glorifying God. This reference is not the only mention of the natural world in the Bible, let alone in the psalms. Read Genesis 1:1–2:4. Note that after God created all of the aforementioned parts of the world, God called them "good." God acknowledged the goodness of the world and the world, in return, acknowledged the goodness of God.

As a group talk about ways in which you recognize the goodness of all God's creation. Discuss harm that has been done to nature by humans and talk about ways in which the faithful can care for creation by affirming its goodness.

In the Rear View

First Chronicles 16 was a response to the manifestation of God's presence, communicated to the people by having the Ark of the Covenant amongst them. The faithful response of the people was to sing.

Singing allows the faithful to articulate and communicate praise for God and celebrates God's relation not only to the covenant community, but the entire creation. The whole world—humans, seas, fish, fields, animals, and trees—all express praise for God's goodness and steadfast love. We are encouraged to join in harmony, with all creation, in praising God.

Day 1:

Verse 36 calls for "families of the peoples" to "ascribe to the Lord." Keeping in mind this inclusive statement, think about communities of people that are different from your community. What are the differences? similarities? What common bonds can you find? Spend some time journaling your thoughts.

Day 2:

Verses 31-33 tell of ways in which parts of the natural world participate in praising God. Take a hike through nature and notice the trees, fields, and animals. When you return, write a prayer of thanks to God for God's creativeness and care for all the creatures.

Day 3:

Reflect about your nature hike yesterday. How did you experience God's presence? God considers creation important enough to take care of it, so we should do no less. Make a list of ways you can join with God in caring for the earth. (Examples: recycling, planting a garden, walking instead of driving when able) Commit to doing at least one of these things.

Day 4:

Read 1 Chronicles 16:34. Offer a prayer of thanksgiving to God and journal about ways in which God has been faithful to you.

Joy in Coming Home

Scripture for lesson:
Isaiah 52:1-12

Written by Marcus Hayes

FAITH LIFE

When I was a child, our family had a cocker spaniel named Kirby. We found Kirby wandering on our farm one day. His wariness of human contact made us think that a previous owner had abused or neglected him. After gentle petting and giving him food, Kirby warmed up to us and became the sixth member of our family. He loved us as much as we loved him.

For Kirby, the downfall to being a dog was that he could not travel with us. When we went on a trip, Kirby was depressed the entire time we were gone. My grandfather took care of him while we were gone. When he fed Kirby, Kirby didn't show any interest in eating. All Kirby wanted to do was lie on the porch, whimper, and look sad and lonely.

Our house sat at the end of a long gravel driveway. Once we turned into the driveway, we could see Kirby in the distance, waiting for us. As soon as he heard and saw the car coming down the road, his head would shoot up. Once he realized that his family was coming home, he would spring to his feet and race down the side of the road to meet our car. Then he would run alongside the car, barking all the way to where we parked. Kirby was so excited to see us that we couldn't get our feet on the ground before he was greeting us by jumping in our laps. It never failed—he would get so excited to see us that he always greeted my dad by uncontrollably urinating on him.

Though he stayed in the physical space that was his home, his family wasn't there. Our return meant that he was now at home with his family. For our family, and for Kirby, it was a homecoming that resulted in unrestrained joy. (Just ask my Dad!)

Prep for the Journey

Isaiah 52:1-12 is part of a much broader text of scripture that arose from Judah's exile in Babylon following the fall and destruc-

> When have you been homesick? How did you feel when you returned home?

When have you felt as if God had abandoned you? How did you respond to this feeling?

When have you received good news? What was it like to wait for the news to come? How did you react when you first heard it?

tion of Jerusalem. When Babylon destroyed Jerusalem in 587 B.C., the Temple was burned to the ground, the Davidic monarchy was overthrown, and many of the people (including the king) were taken captive and scattered throughout the Babylonian Empire. It marked the end of Judah as an independent nation-state, leaving the covenant community to wonder if they, as God's chosen people, had been abandoned by God. (The pain of these events is expressed in laments that can be found in Lamentations and Psalms, such as Psalm 137.)

Prophets such as Jeremiah, Ezekiel, and Isaiah broadly claimed that the exile was the result of Israel and Judah's sin. In general, these prophets asserted that the people neglected their covenant relationship with God, choosing to offer their worship and allegiance to idols. The prophets maintained that though the consequences of such actions were harsh, God would remain faithful and bring restoration.

This theme of anticipation is picked up in the latter chapters of Isaiah, who prophesied a message of hope: the people who were displaced would soon have a homecoming. Isaiah proclaimed that God was at work in the midst of human history to bring about a new thing, a restoration for those who had suffered in exile. This restoration was articulated in terms of a renewed Holy City in which the people would be at home with their land, their community, and their God. Help was on the way! Rejoice!

On the Road

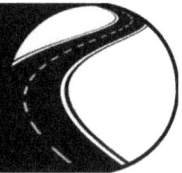

Read Isaiah 52:1-2.
Awake, awake,
*   put on your strength, O Zion!*
Put on your beautiful garments,
*   O Jerusalem, the holy city;*
for the uncircumcised and the unclean
*   shall enter you no more.*
² Shake yourself from the dust, rise up,
*   O captive Jerusalem;*
loose the bonds from your neck,
*   O captive daughter Zion!*

Like excited children wanting their parents to get up on Christmas morning, the prophet had an exciting message for a city held in captivity: "Awake, awake, put on your strength, O Zion!" God is up to something and the holy city must arise to the new day that is dawning. The prophet was speaking of Jerusalem, but throughout the text the prophet also referred to the city as *Zion*, which is an alternative name for Jerusalem, the Temple, and the people of God. It is used poetically to designate the city and the people's special relationship to God.

Although the statement that the "uncircumcised and unclean" will not again enter the city seems harsh and inhospitable, it was a reference to Jerusalem's destruction. The city and its holy objects had been defiled by enemies who came in and "stretched their hands over all precious things" (Lamentations 1:10). Jerusalem had become a place where "the blood of the righteous" was shed (Lamentations 4:13). Zion had been held captive, and God's presence appeared to be gone.

But now she [the city] can shake off the dust, loose the bonds, rise up, and put on her beautiful dress because God is going to rejuvenate her. God has not forgotten Zion and her people. Out of God's faithfulness and love, God is about to do something new for those who have suffered.

Read Isaiah 52:3-6.

For thus says the LORD: You were sold for nothing, and you shall be redeemed without money. ⁴ For thus says the Lord GOD: Long ago, my people went down into Egypt to reside there as aliens; the Assyrian, too, has oppressed them without cause. ⁵ Now therefore what am I doing here, says the LORD, seeing that my people are taken away without cause? Their rulers howl, says the LORD, and continually, all day long, my name is despised. ⁶ Therefore my people shall know my name; therefore in that day they shall know that it is I who speak; here am I.

People have noted that Israel being sold "for nothing" should be understood as being sold without cause or justification. God acknowledged the lack of justification in the harsh judgment that Israel had suffered throughout its history, whether it was slavery in Egypt or suffering at the hands of the Assyrians. God's people had endured their share of oppressive circumstances, which had come to include being exiled and held captive by Babylon. Yet, just as it was in the past, so it will be again. Even though Israel's captors despised the name of the Lord, God would redeem the people and vindicate God's name. Because God was going to deliver them, the people acknowledged and praised God's name on the other side of their current affliction.

Those who are presently suffering can trust this proclamation and have faith that God will bring them deliverance. Such faith is not blind faith or a pipe dream hoping in "what ifs," but is rooted in the declaration of God who has a history of redeeming Israel. Because of what God has done in the past, God can be trusted in the present to open up a future of newness and salvation. Zion's renewed hope is grounded in its past experience of being treasured and redeemed by God.

Read Isaiah 52:7-12.
How beautiful upon the mountains
        are the feet of the messenger who announces peace,
who brings good news,
        who announces salvation,
        who says to Zion, "Your God reigns."
⁸ Listen! Your sentinels lift up their voices,

When have you seen or experienced God "doing something new?" What changes resulted?

How does past experience influence trust? How does knowing that God has a history of being present and active in the lives of those who suffer affect your ability to trust that God hears you?

together they sing for joy;
for in plain sight they see
    the return of the LORD to Zion.
⁹ Break forth together into singing,
    you ruins of Jerusalem;
for the LORD has comforted his people,
    he has redeemed Jerusalem.
¹⁰ The LORD has bared his holy arm
    before the eyes of all the nations;
and all the ends of the earth shall see
    the salvation of our God.

¹¹ Depart, depart, go out from there!
    Touch no unclean thing;
go out from the midst of it, purify yourselves,
    you who carry the vessels of the LORD.
¹² For you shall not go out in haste,
    and you shall not go in flight;
for the LORD will go before you,
    and the God of Israel will be your rear guard.

Can feet really be beautiful?! If they are bringing good news and giving life they can! This poetic description fills our imaginations with heralds running over mountains and fighting a loss of breath to deliver the good tidings of peace to Zion. The good news, the announcement of salvation, is expressed by the proclamation: "Your God reigns!" This statement is not only about God, but also about Babylon and her gods. It was believed that when one nation conquered another it was the result of the conquering nation's god being more powerful than the god of the conquered. By stating "your God reigns!" the herald was proclaiming that all the forces that oppressed and caused the people to suffer were not greater than the God who was delivering them. This jubilant event caused the city's watchmen to erupt with songs of joy.

As a poet, Isaiah let us know that the joyful singing was not restricted to any one group, or humans for that matter. In 52:9 the ruins of Jerusalem—the very places that were destroyed, abandoned, and forgotten—join in the chorus. This imagery affirmed the healing power of God and God's ability to return something to wholeness. The areas that had been harmed and destroyed had become joyous sanctuaries testifying to the goodness of God. In this passage Isaiah offered another biblical example of God working through brokenness to accomplish that which is holy and life-giving.

God's comforting presence and redemption affect all areas of destruction and bring joy to all creation. As 52:10 states "all the ends of the earth shall see the salvation of our God." The restoration of Jerusalem was done for the well-being of the people, but it also served the larger mission of God to minister to and redeem the world. In 52:11-12 Israel was summoned toward a homecoming. It was announced that the exiles would make their journey back to Jerusalem and God

When do you sing? What might cause you randomly to start singing praise to God?

When have you seen God use something broken, forgotten, or neglected to bring about goodness, beauty, or joy?

48

would watch over them, much like God watched over their ancestors as they wandered in the wilderness.

God had a history of such provision, thus God could be trusted to do it again. Isaiah proclaimed a new thing that God was doing to bring the exiles home. In the midst of their abandonment, in their "home-sickness," the people of God received the good news of redemption and a way home. Their immediate response was to sing with joy.

Scenic Route

Though this scripture is in the Old Testament, and refers specifically to the experience of exile, its themes of captivity, redemption, and joy are expressed in the mission of Christ. As Christians, we affirm that the entire creation is in bondage to sin and death. The good news is that Jesus is the source of our salvation. Through his life, death, and resurrection we are redeemed from sin and made new. As John 3:16 informs us, our redemption comes about because "God so loved the world."

The apostle Paul picked up on this redemption and articulated it in his correspondence with the church in Corinth: "So if anyone is in Christ, there is a new creation: everything old has passed away; see, everything has become new! All this is from God, who reconciled us to himself through Christ, and has given us the ministry of reconciliation; that is, in Christ God was reconciling the world to himself, not counting their trespasses against them, and entrusting the message of reconciliation to us" (2 Corinthians 5:17-19).

For those who suffer from the effects of sin and separation, God is at work in Christ to "make all things new." This message is not isolated to ancient Israelites. It is good news to all who long for redemption out of the brokenness of their lives. As we see in Isaiah, God's efforts toward reconciliation and newness are able to take root and flourish within every part of creation.

Workers Ahead

Isaiah 52 arises from and speaks to a community that has suffered greatly from displacement and oppression. It would be naïve to read this text and not consider the millions of modern-day refugees and communities of people suffering from oppression. Isaiah, much like

What moments in your life have brought you the most joy? What was it about this situation that brought you joy? How did you express that joy?

What does reconciliation mean to you? What does it mean to be reconciled to God? to one another? to creation? Why is God's act of reconciliation good news?

How can you bring comfort to those suffering from homelessness in your community? How might you offer relief to those in your town who have little or no food? What can your community do to show hospitality to refugees, locally and abroad?

Jesus, was intent on offering "good news" to these people in the form of relief, comfort, and peace so that those who are grieved can experience joy and know that God cares for them.

Discuss with your group ways in which your church can participate in ministries to those who are oppressed. Although you will not solve every problem, pray that the Holy Spirit will guide you toward participating in a particular ministry or advocacy. May our words and our actions proclaim to all people: "God reigns!"

In the Rear View

Situated within a lonely and oppressive exile, Isaiah urged those in captivity to be prepared because God was bringing them good news of a homecoming. This act of God created a new situation, yet it was rooted in God's previous activity to save and liberate. Thus, all of us who suffer from oppression and brokenness can trust that God will meet us in our mess to offer us redemption and salvation. This unexpected good news is a source of pure joy. All we have left to do is offer praises to God.

Travel Log

Day 1:

Isaiah asserted that Judah's homecoming and the restoration of Jerusalem was purely an act of God. Spend time in prayer reflecting upon God's actions in your life. Write down these instances, giving thanks to God for each one.

Day 2:

Because God acted to redeem the people, Isaiah could not help but testify to this experience of God's goodness. Write an informal testimony that you can share with someone, either personally or through social media. Use your experience to encourage someone else so that "all... shall see the salvation of our God."

Day 3:

    Isaiah articulated that the purest expression of joy in response to God is to sing. Write down a verse to your favorite hymn of praise or the words of a praise song (Flip through a hymnal or search online, if necessary). Sing this verse as a thanksgiving to God and an expression of the joy God has brought you.

Day 4:

    Isaiah wrote "How beautiful upon the mountains are the feet of the messenger who announces peace." Who has brought you good news, either by words or actions? Jot down some of their names. Write one or more of these people a note to thank them for allowing God to use them in your life.

Day 5:

This text was directed to people who had suffered displacement and oppression. Who are these people today? If you have trouble naming them, do an Internet search for stories of oppressed communities. List these peoples and situations below. Pray that God will send comfort and peace to these peoples.

Day 6:

Move your prayers into action. If you are able, become involved with an organization that provides relief to those who are suffering from disaster or displacement. You may be able to work with this organization or make a donation to their efforts. You could also volunteer at a ministry that serves the marginalized of your community, such as a food pantry or an after-school program for impoverished students.

Day 7:

In Romans 10:15 Paul quoted Isaiah 52:7 and urged the faithful to announce salvation in Christ to all people, not just a limited few. Read Romans 10:5-15. What do you think Paul meant when he stated "there is no distinction between Jew and Greek; the same Lord is Lord of all and generous to all"? Journal your thoughts about the good news of Jesus, good news that does not discriminate.

Joy in the Shared Life

Scripture for lesson:
Luke 1:24-25, 39-45

Written by Tiffany Hall McClung

I recently found myself saying to a couple of mothers of my daughter's friends, "I hope they are friends for a very long time." This desire is something that I didn't quite understand about parenthood until I found myself in the middle of it. The desire for my children to "find their people" is stronger than I ever thought it would be. I think about my own relationships; those that are most precious to me are the ones that are filled with shared experiences over the course of half a lifetime.

It never ceases to amaze me that when I am with these long-time friends, our shared history is so strong that it almost becomes another person. I enjoy hearing my mom talk about her shared life with her two best friends, friends she met when she was five years old, friends with whom she still has sleep-overs even as they live into their mid-seventies. They have been together through births of children, grandchildren, and great grandchildren. They have been together through the deaths of a son and of each of their husbands. They talk on the phone daily and they share everything. Whether it is my daughter and her 10-year-old friends, my mother and her 70-year-old friends, or myself with my middle-aged friends, the common factor is joy in the shared life.

Prep for the Journey

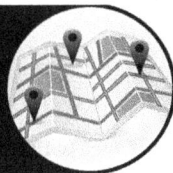

Read Luke 1:24-25.

After those days his wife Elizabeth conceived, and for five months she remained in seclusion. She said, ^{25} "This is what the Lord has done for me when he looked favorably on me and took away the disgrace I have endured among my people."

This week's lesson revolves around what has become known as "the visitation." Luke tells us that Elizabeth and Zechariah were old and had not conceived any children, that "Elizabeth was barren." If

Note from author: This lesson deals with Elizabeth and Mary during their pregnancies, which can be a sensitive matter for women who either have chosen not to have children or who suffer infertility. It is my hope that all women are welcomed into our communities without experiencing the shame Elizabeth had to endure.

How do you react to people who choose not to have children or who have been unable to do so? How are these families treated differently in society? the church? In what ways can the church make them feel welcome and fully included in the community?

What do you think about people who choose to have children late in life? Why?

When have you felt left out of the community? In what ways do you see God working in your life to heal those experiences?

blame were to be attached to the problem of childlessness, there was no question that the woman must bear it. Of course, this attitude was not unusual for women of this time in history. It was their duty to produce children for their husbands, and sons were expected. So, while there would have been a great deal of shame for Zechariah, the bulk of the weight fell onto Elizabeth's shoulders.

And then the unexpected happened. An angel appeared to Zechariah and told him that his wife was going to have a son, saying "You will have joy and gladness, and many will rejoice at his birth." God broke open an impossible situation for this couple and brought joy into the midst of it.

Based on what we know of the culture at the time, we can assume life was not particularly easy for Elizabeth. She would have been an outcast in her own community. Others would have considered her barrenness to be God's punishment; there was no other logical reason for it. Elizabeth would have had a lonely existence, one lacking the shared life to which God calls us. The community would have manifested its reproach in a variety of ways, ways that excluded Elizabeth from her own community, which we can assume from her reaction in verse 25: "[the Lord] took away the disgrace I have endured among my people."

So why did Elizabeth remain secluded for five months? She may have been afraid that something would go wrong. Perhaps she had endured miscarriages before. Perhaps she wanted to be absolutely certain this pregnancy would reach full term before letting the community know. It would have been terribly painful to be brought back into a community only to be rejected once again.

The next time we see Elizabeth in the scriptures is when Mary, a relative of hers, comes for a visit. Mary, of course, had experienced quite a surprise of her own. An angel had visited her, explaining that she would have a child. She was not old and she was not married, yet she was chosen. While receiving this news, the angel informed Mary that Elizabeth was in her sixth month of pregnancy. This news seems to have been given as proof that God can do what seems to be impossible.

We don't know if Mary understood that Elizabeth and Zechariah had been told their son would usher in a new world and prepare people to meet the Messiah. We can assume, though, that Mary felt a kinship with Elizabeth that went beyond family ties. In what seems to be her first act following the news that she was pregnant with the Messiah, Mary sought the companionship of someone who would understand. She and Elizabeth were having similar experiences, and Mary needed to be with her.

On the Road

Read Luke 1:39-41.

In those days Mary set out and went with haste to a Judean town in the hill country, ⁴⁰ where she entered the house of Zechariah and greeted Elizabeth. 41 When Elizabeth heard Mary's greeting, the child leaped in her womb. And Elizabeth was filled with the Holy Spirit.

It was very important for Mary to get to Elizabeth, even though it seems that, other than being pregnant, the two women had very little in common. However, once they were together, we learn how important this shared experience was. Elizabeth told Mary that "the child in my womb leaped for joy" at being near Jesus. The thought of John understanding, even in the womb, that he was in the presence of the Messiah is powerful.

Mary and Elizabeth were not ignorant women. They likely had some idea of how important these two children would be. However, it is also likely that fully understanding what each one held in her womb was impossible. How could one understand this completely? Being the parent of your every day, average child is beyond understanding! So, how could Mary and Elizabeth have fully grasped the magnitude of that of which they were a part?

Even so, they understood that each of them was part of something larger than themselves. They also understood that they were sharing an experience and a history that only they could understand. Mary traveled "with haste" to Elizabeth because there is joy in shared experiences. She needed to be with "her people." Elizabeth embraced her for the same reasons. We can assume that Luke included the statement of John leaping in the womb for that reason as well. Jesus and John were sharing an experience, a history, through their mothers, a history that would lead them to shared experiences of baptism, preaching, and martyrdom. There is great joy in a shared life with Jesus.

Scenic Route

Read Luke 1:42-45.

And Elizabeth was filled with the Holy Spirit ⁴² and exclaimed with a loud cry, "Blessed are you among women, and blessed is the fruit of your womb. ⁴³ And why has this happened to me, that the mother of my Lord comes to me? ⁴⁴ For as soon as I heard the sound of your greeting,

With whom have you developed a stronger relationship because of shared experiences? If not for those experiences, how likely is it that you would have had a relationship with that person?

How have shared experiences and history shaped you into the person you are now? Who are your people today? Who is your community? Who are those with whom you long to be when important moments are happening in your life?

the child in my womb leaped for joy. [45] And blessed is she who believed that there would be a fulfillment of what was spoken to her by the Lord."

Elizabeth amazes me. Put yourself in her sandals for a moment. Her young, pregnant, unmarried relative arrived unexpectedly at her door. In those days, being pregnant and unmarried was grounds for stoning a woman. Many people would have turned her away, not wanting to be shamed by her situation. Elizabeth probably had lots of questions about this unexpected visit, but before she could ask any of them, the Holy Spirit came upon her and she began to rejoice.

The Holy Spirit allowed Elizabeth to know the reasons for Mary's visit and about the child she was carrying. Elizabeth's spontaneous praise included how blessed Mary was, but then it became more about how blessed Elizabeth was to have Mary visit her. Elizabeth saw herself as favored to have been invited to share this moment with Mary. She was filled with joy, just as was her own unborn son, to be sharing the experience with Mary, with Jesus, and with God.

Elizabeth joyfully blessed Mary rather than turning her away. Her blessing was two-fold. First, she blessed the mother of Jesus for being chosen. It was a blessing simply for God to have chosen Mary for such a task. Second, she blessed Mary for believing the word of God. Elizabeth understood how easily Mary, though chosen, could have been unbelieving and walked away from the task. Elizabeth understood who Mary was and the ways in which she had been blessed.

It was the joy of John in the womb that caused Elizabeth to understand that Mary was "the mother of my Lord." John's reaction gave her an understanding of how big this moment was for them all. Elizabeth praised God for the shared experience, for the shared history, and for Mary's faithfulness as the chosen vessel for the Messiah.

Workers Ahead

This encounter between Mary and Elizabeth leads us to understand the importance of having someone with whom to share our experiences and history. Mary probably had other friends to whom she could have turned, but she chose Elizabeth. In part, her choice was because they were both pregnant and, in part, it was because the angel had mentioned Elizabeth as an example of the impossible things God can do. Elizabeth was also older, which presumes a certain wisdom that Mary likely lacked. We do not have the stories of the three months Mary spent with Elizabeth, but we can presume that Elizabeth shared many important things with her during that time.

We need a community with whom we share our lives. Our shared history brings joy and helps us to make decisions. It is important for us to reflect on those with whom we share this life, this history. Some of them may be older. Some of them will be younger.

As a class, name some of the older members of your faith community who enable the community to live a strong, shared life. Be specific about the ways in which they offer wisdom to the community.

Now, name some of the younger folks who do the same. How is God calling you to serve the younger? Be specific about the ways they enable the shared history of the congregation to continue.

Throughout the coming week, write notes to those the group identified. You may want to decide as a group who will write to whom, or you may just want to flood the mailboxes (or inboxes) of each person. Let them know that they bring you joy and that you ask God's blessings for them.

In the Rear View

The encounter between Mary and Elizabeth was also the first meeting between John and Jesus. We know that the two women were relatives, though we have no knowledge of how close they had been. We also know that Mary traveled some distance to the countryside in order to visit Elizabeth.

One was older and married to a priest. She had lived with infertility, which made her an outcast among her own community. The other was likely a young teenager, and unmarried. We assume that before the angel's visit she had lived a normal life in her community.

Shared experiences and a shared history brought them together. Mary longed to be with someone who would understand what she was experiencing. Elizabeth rejoiced at being invited into the Messianic journey. John, from the womb, leaped with delight at being near the Messiah. The joy that each of them felt was God-given through a shared life. This joy would have been impossible if each of them had remained secluded. Shared life experiences and history binds people together and provides for some of the deepest moments of joy we can obtain. Even more important, though, is being invited to share in God's work. Mary, Elizabeth, and John rejoiced because they each had been invited into the shared work of God, through the Christ, on earth. That joy cannot be outdone.

In what ways have others caused you to want to leap for joy?

Why do you think this encounter was included in the Gospel of Luke? What are the most important parts of this particular story? Who is the main character?

Day 1:

Find a quiet place that has no distractions. Take this book, a pen, and a Bible and go to that place. Slowly read Luke 1:24-25, 39-45. Set a timer for 5 minutes and sit silently listening for God to reveal to you a word or phrase from the scripture. You may need to read the scripture more than once. Breathe deeply and in rhythm as you simply sit in the presence of God repeating the word or phrase.

When the 5 minutes has ended, set the timer again for 5 minutes. Now write about your experience. Read what you have written at the end of the 5 minutes. Reflect on what surprised you.

Day 2:

Think of one of your oldest and dearest friends and write a note to him or her. You may or may not choose to send the note, but write it as if you will. Share some of your memories from your shared history. Let the person know the things for which you are most thankful. Pray for your friend.

Day 3:

Gather old newspapers, magazines, scissors, tape/glue stick, markers, and a piece of paper. Pick a place to work where you have time to reflect without distraction. Ask God to reveal to you the ways in which you have participated in God's work throughout your life. From the magazine and newspapers, cut out images that represent these ways. Create a collage of the shared history you have with God. You may also want to draw or write scriptures or other words on your sheet of paper. Allow yourself the time and space to be creative. Once you have completed your collage, take time to look at it closely. Thank God for allowing you to be part of God's work in the world.

Day 4:

Write one or more prayers for the people you identified during the group time. (See "In the Rear View.") Be specific in your prayers. Ask God's blessings on those individual who share their wisdom with your community.

Day 5:

Much has been written about John knowing the Messiah before either of them was even born. What do you think? Put into your own words what it means that John leaped with joy when Elizabeth heard Mary's voice.

Day 6:

This whole week has been about the joy of the shared life, in particular the shared life among those who have a shared history. Call someone and meet for a meal today. Share your life. Celebrate your history. Thank God for your time together. Afterward, journal about the time you spent with this person.

Day 7:

Read Luke 1:24-25, 39-45 again. Now read it a second time more slowly. Breathe deeply and take in every word as you read the passage. Write down images, words, or phrases that jump out at you. Thank God for a good week. Rest as you know that in God there is great joy.

Joy in the Big Picture

Scripture for lesson:
1 Samuel 2:1-10; Luke 1:46-56

Written by Tiffany Hall McClung

How easy is it for you to see the big picture?

As I write this lesson, I am mere weeks from celebrating my 25th wedding anniversary. Walking down the aisle at 18 years old did not provide for a good view of the big picture. In fact, my view of the world was as narrow as the white paper runner upon which I walked. Living through difficult times, death of loved ones, and the terrifying and overwhelming love of raising children together has widened that picture a great deal.

At 18, the term "help-mate" made me laugh. I couldn't see how that fit into the picture. In my forties, I love that term so much. My spouse is my help-mate; without his help I wouldn't know what to do. I hope I am helpful to him, too. Our life together is helping one another navigate career, parenthood, and relationships. Some of my most joyous times are when he allows me to help him with a particular problem or task. To be invited into the work he is doing, to be allowed to participate, and to make a difference in that work brings me great joy. Joy comes from being in the big picture.

Prep for the Journey

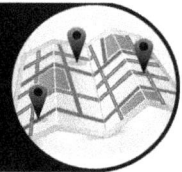

Read 1 Samuel 2:1-10.
Hannah prayed and said,
"My heart exults in the Lord;
*   my strength is exalted in my God.*
My mouth derides my enemies,
*   because I rejoice in my victory.*
2 "There is no Holy One like the Lord,
*   no one besides you;*
*   there is no Rock like our God.*
3 Talk no more so very proudly,
*   let not arrogance come from your mouth;*
for the Lord is a God of knowledge,

and by him actions are weighed.
[4] *The bows of the mighty are broken,*
but the feeble gird on strength.
[5] *Those who were full have hired themselves out for bread,*
but those who were hungry are fat with spoil.
The barren has borne seven,
but she who has many children is forlorn.
[6] *The Lord kills and brings to life;*
he brings down to Sheol and raises up.
[7] *The Lord makes poor and makes rich;*
he brings low, he also exalts.
[8] *He raises up the poor from the dust;*
he lifts the needy from the ash heap,
to make them sit with princes
and inherit a seat of honor.
For the pillars of the earth are the Lord's,
and on them he has set the world.
[9] *"He will guard the feet of his faithful ones,*
but the wicked shall be cut off in darkness;
for not by might does one prevail.
[10] *The Lord! His adversaries shall be shattered;*
the Most High will thunder in heaven.
The Lord will judge the ends of the earth;
he will give strength to his king,
and exalt the power of his anointed."

This lesson explores what has become known as "The Magnificat" (Latin for magnifies) or "Mary's Song." Mary's song appears only in Luke's Gospel and has become well known among Christians. Most of us could quote the first line of the song, and often do around Christmas: "My soul magnifies the Lord, and my spirit rejoices in God my savior."

Before we spend time looking at Mary's song, it is important to recognize its history. Most scholars agree that this passage has its roots in the song that Hannah sang after the birth of Samuel (1 Samuel 2:1-10). Her song was clearly a blueprint for the mother of Jesus, who would have known Hannah's song as well as we know Mary's.

It is common for Luke's narrative to allude to Hebrew Scriptures. For the writer of Luke, it was important to bring to mind the old, old stories from scripture as the new stories were being told. Fred Craddock writes, "To say that these new stories are old stories is not simply to say that they are patterned after Old Testament records; rather, it is to say that the writer apparently assumed that the readers would recognize the old in the new." Mary's song, then, not only points us toward the birth of Jesus, but also causes us to reflect on the work of God throughout the history of God's people. The joy expressed through this song is not confined to one particular moment, but calls to mind the work of God throughout history. In other words, it calls us to look at the big picture.

In what ways do you pattern your prayers after familiar scriptures or even hymns? In what ways does Mary's song challenge your prayer life?

When do you find it helpful to recall old stories? Why?

On the Road

Read Luke 1:46-49.

And Mary said,
"My soul magnifies the Lord,
    ⁴⁷ and my spirit rejoices in God my Savior,
⁴⁸ for he has looked with favor on the lowliness of his servant.
    Surely, from now on all generations will call me blessed;
⁴⁹ for the Mighty One has done great things for me,
    and holy is his name.
⁵⁰ His mercy is for those who fear him
    from generation to generation.

We can imagine Mary, a young teenage girl, going about her normal chores when the angel Gabriel personally delivered a message from God. Instead of reacting with doubt and fear, Mary humbly accepted Gabriel's message. We get a little bit of a clue about her feelings in that she seems to have left to visit her cousin, Elizabeth, fairly soon after the delivery of the message.

It was likely that Mary was aware of Elizabeth's infertility. Considering such, Gabriel told her of Elizabeth's pregnancy as proof that nothing is impossible with God. So, it is not surprising that Mary went to visit Elizabeth. While we don't know many of the details about this visit, suffice it to say that there was much rejoicing. From that rejoicing, Mary's joy was such that she couldn't contain it in mere prose. She burst into poetry and sang about what God was doing in her life and the lives of those around her.

Mary began with the narrow picture. Using the personal pronoun she simply stated the joy she was feeling for God and God's decision to choose her for this purpose. It is no surprise that she would rely on the Hebrew Scriptures for a blueprint of how to speak (or sing) about this monumental event. How could any of us know what to say about a wonderful and terrifying gift like this? To think that Mary was a young girl amplifies this seemingly impossible moment that has been made evident by God.

Mary very quickly turned to the bigger picture, though. Her song is not about herself, but about the work God was doing for God's people—not only in the present, but throughout the past and into the future. "His mercy is for those who fear him from generation to generation" is the turning point in what could be described as the beginning of the second stanza. Mary used one of four "verses" to praise God for what God was doing in her life. The remaining three verses focus on the big picture—what God was doing in the lives of the oppressed and what God would do for God's people in the future. In the same way that Hannah thanked God for Samuel while praying for the larger community, Mary's words draw our attention to the bigger picture.

How might you have reacted to the news Mary received? How do you think her immediate family felt? With whom would you have shared this news?

What would change in our churches if we spent 3/4 of our time on the bigger picture? How might our Advent and Christmas celebrations change if we quoted the other three verses of Mary's song as much as we do the first one? How does focusing more attention on the beginning words of her song than on the bigger picture of God's work in the world cause us to miss important points?

Read Luke 1:51-55.

He has shown strength with his arm;
    he has scattered the proud in the thoughts of their hearts.
[52] *He has brought down the powerful from their thrones,*
    and lifted up the lowly;
[53] *he has filled the hungry with good things,*
    and sent the rich away empty.
[54] *He has helped his servant Israel,*
    in remembrance of his mercy,
[55] *according to the promise he made to our ancestors,*
    to Abraham and to his descendants forever."

The similarities to Hannah's prayer continue with the reversals of fortune as Mary's song expands from a personal praise to the big picture. Luke's Gospel is full of these reversals of fortune. When using that term, we mean the ways in which those who are "high" are brought "low" and vice versa. It is not surprising that the Gospel of Luke focuses on this paradigm since Luke was the Gentile among the Gospel writers. His writing is a testimony to the ways in which God includes those upon whom others look down. For Luke, it was important to note that God's favor rests on the "least of these."

From the moment the angel appeared to Zechariah and Elizabeth (the first verses of the book), it is clear that the good news was being brought to those whom the world would rather forget. As we have read about the birth of Jesus in our over 2000 years of history, it may seem commonplace that an angel appeared to a young, unmarried girl and that God chose this girl to usher the Christ into the world. Perhaps we forget that the Christ could have come into the world in all manner of ways, thus causing us to overlook the scandal, but it was not lost on Mary. She was well aware that God's choice of her was an upset to the worldly order of kings and kingdoms and her song expressed this awareness.

Mary lived in a world that preached shame and honor to her day in and day out. It is a miracle that she could see what God was doing in and through her and throughout history in the midst of that belief system. What the church and culture said was that God would never choose a girl for anything, much less an important task such as bringing the Christ into the world. The religious and cultural standards dictated that an unmarried, pregnant girl brought shame to everyone around her and that she should be disowned and cast out. Accordingly, Mary had nothing about which to sing praises, nor should she even have had the nerve to approach God with such a song.

It is a miracle that Mary could see the big picture when narrow mindedness was the order of the day. Instead of allowing the accept-

Where do you see God at work in reversing the status quo? In what ways can you participate in that work?

What does it mean for us that the Christ was brought into the world through a scandalous and shameful girl?

In what ways do our churches and culture continue to perpetuate shame and honor? Where do you see those who are doing God's work being shamed?

ed norms to prevail, Mary sang about her joy in being chosen by God. She sang about the ways in which God had reversed the status quo and was using her as an example of that reversal. She also sings about "the triumph of God's purposes for all people everywhere" (Craddock). Much of Mary's song focused on the big picture, a picture that is big enough for all of us, a picture that shows the oppressed being freed.

Workers Ahead

The Magnificat automatically calls to mind "song." It is Mary's song of praise to God, which appears to have been spontaneous. In today's culture, such spontaneous outbursts of joy are often viewed with skepticism, and possibly with reproach. Consider the reaction if Mary had been in your worship service and this song had come pouring forth.

Take a look at some of the hymns and songs your faith community uses regularly. Consider whether they focus on the individual or have a broader focus. Many of our beliefs are influenced by the songs and hymns we learn and sing at church. Talk together about some of the images and understandings related to your faith that have come from hymns.

"Being narrow-minded" is a comment often tossed about when groups or individuals do not see the other's point of view. Sometimes the failure is because one or both is too focused on how the issue will directly affect him or her rather than on how it will affect everyone. Mary understood that God was doing something very special. She didn't get caught up in what the reality would mean for her personally, but readily put her own needs aside so that God's purpose could be achieved.

It is usually really easy to see when others have a narrow focus. However, it can be much more difficult to see and confess our own narrow mindedness. Ask God to help you see the bigger picture and to show you specific ways to be part of the work God is doing in the world.

Since the church is comprised of people, it can also become narrow minded. Reflect as to how your congregation has been, is, or might be headed for narrow mindedness. Talk about ways you can begin to see and relate to the world through the bigger picture of God's work in the world.

In what situations do you need to set aside your needs so that God's purpose can be more easily achieved?

How do you deal with those who are narrow-minded? How can you avoid being narrow-minded?

In the Rear View

The Magnificat may be one of the best and most classic examples of praise in our scriptures. Mary's joy in what God was doing in her life and the lives of her people was clear from the first words out of her mouth. Mary's song is not just about herself in the present moment, but is about God's relationship with God's people throughout all time. Evidence of this focus is found in the ways her song echoed Hannah's as well as the fact that Elizabeth's pregnancy with John was intimately connected to Mary. In other words, there is a progression and connection throughout history to what God is doing through God's people.

The writer of Luke draws our attention to the ways in which God has been at work throughout history and reminds us that God will continue to be at work throughout the future. As Fred Craddock notes, "So sure is the singer that God will do what is promised that it is proclaimed as accomplished fact." Furthermore, this relationship between God and God's people often reverses what our culture (and church) says about the world order. Through Mary's words (and Hannah's before her), we are reminded that God will take the lowest of the low and lift them high. Mary used herself as an example of this very thing being done.

Reflecting on your relationship with God, how do you see the big picture?

How does it feel to realize that what God did in Mary's time is connected to us and that what God does now will be connected to future generations?

Day 1:

Write the word *magnify* on an index card or small piece of paper. Place it in a prominent spot where you will see it several times during the day. Each time you notice the word, pause and thank God for three things: one from the past, one from the present, and one thing that you anticipate in the future.

Day 2:

Write a song or poem. Use Hannah's and Mary's as templates, but write about what God is doing in your life. Consider the big picture as you write. In what ways can you see your own relationship with God connected to the wider community, even throughout history?

Day 3:

Find three or four images you can look at and reflect upon. It really doesn't matter what the image is because you want to look at perspective. What is the central focus of the image? Does it focus on a narrow subject or is there a wide perspective? As you do this exercise, be open for the ways in which God will show you new perspectives of the big picture. Journal about your experience. In what ways have these images enabled you to meditate on God's big picture?

Day 4:

Identify a relatively small object in your house or office on which to focus. Stare at the object for a while and sketch it in the space below, using as much detail as possible. Leave lots of white space around the sketch of the object. As you sketch, ask God to reveal places in your life where you have a narrow view.

Day 5:

Using the same location as for Day 4, focus on the same object again, except broaden your focus to include the area around it. Begin to fill in the details on your previous sketch. What is next to the object? How big is it compared to the things around it? Sketch the bigger picture as you ask God to broaden your own perspective in your relationship with God.

Day 6:

Go for a walk, taking in as many of the details in your surroundings as possible. See your neighborhood or the space around your workplace in a new way. Look beyond where the sidewalk ends and take in the big picture. Thank God for everything you see and hear and feel and smell. Take a selfie to commemorate your walk, but make sure that your face is only a small part of the bigger picture! Once you have returned, journal about your experience.

Day 7:

God is still in the business of reversing the status quo; at times using us to do so. Identify situations that need to be reversed, those where oppression and other issues are affecting people. List some possible ways you can work with God to accomplish the needed changes.

Sources Cited:
Craddock, Fred. "Luke 1:5-56" *Luke: Interpretation: A Bible Commentary for Teaching and Preaching.* Louisville: John Knox, 1990. 23-30. Print.

Joy in Setting the Stage

Scripture for lesson:
John 2:1-11

Written by Tiffany Hall McClung

In addition to writing curriculum and serving as Chaplain/Director of Theology and Arts at Memphis Theological Seminary, I sometimes work as a stage manager for a local theatre company. It isn't an easy job. It entails a lot of moving parts and, generally speaking, the applause at the end of the show does not include me. And, I love it.

There is a certain excitement in the hour just before the show begins. During this hour, I am usually sweeping the floor, placing set pieces where they need to be, checking that the lights all work, and starting music to welcome the audience. I also check with the actors to be sure they have their props and costumes and keep track of the time so that the actors are where they need to be when they need to be there. In other words, I set the stage. I do my best to make sure everything is ready so that when the actors come onto the stage, everything will go well and they and the audience will have what they need for the best possible experience. If I do my job well, I slip into the dark booth and no one really knows I've been there. There is joy in setting the stage for others to do what they do best.

Prep for the Journey

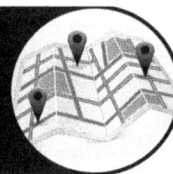

Read John 2:1-4.

On the third day there was a wedding in Cana of Galilee, and the mother of Jesus was there. [2] Jesus and his disciples had also been invited to the wedding. [3] When the wine gave out, the mother of Jesus said to him, "They have no wine." [4] And Jesus said to her, "Woman, what concern is that to you and to me? My hour has not yet come."

The Gospel of John has long been debated. Of the four Gospels, scholars debated the most as to whether or not John should be included in the canon of biblical texts. Since its inclusion, the contrasts between John and the other three Gospels have been clear and the cause of much discussion. While the synoptic Gospels relay events

In what instances do you enjoy setting the stage for others?

What might have caused you to vote for or against the inclusion of John's Gospel in the biblical canon?

in the life of Jesus, the writer of John set out to persuade the reader. Of course, this was also done by relaying events, but it is evident from chapter one that John is different. Metaphorical and symbolic language calls to mind a poet, and the Gospel begins by drawing our attention all the way back to Genesis, "In the beginning." The writer of John was a storyteller who used a well-crafted technique to prove that one must make a choice—either choose the light and follow Jesus or choose the darkness and face condemnation.

The scripture for this lesson continues to illuminate the ways in which John is different. Without much delay, John tells a story about Jesus attending a wedding with his mother. Immediately following the Baptizer's proclamations about Jesus and the recruitment of the first disciples, the reader is dropped into this wedding. We can't help but wonder why the writer chose to share this story at the beginning of Jesus' ministry. It may have been because Jesus performed the first of "his signs," but even so, the so-called miracle of continuing a party to avoid embarrassing a groom still seems an odd choice. Not so for John. He told the story of the Christ in large, thematic units; individual occurrences in the life of Jesus illustrate those units. This story is one such occurrence.

In the Gospel of John, Mary was only known as "the mother of Jesus." This text tells us how she set the stage for what would become Jesus' first miracle in John's telling. Mary called Jesus' attention to the fact that the wine had run out. She was knowingly prodding Jesus to make it right even after Jesus all but said to her, "Butt out, Mom!" She paid no attention to his response! Mary knew how to set a stage, and she did her job well.

On the Road

Read John 1:5-8.

His mother said to the servants, "Do whatever he tells you." ⁶ Now standing there were six stone water jars for the Jewish rites of purification, each holding twenty or thirty gallons. ⁷ Jesus said to them, "Fill the jars with water." And they filled them up to the brim. ⁸ He said to them, "Now draw some out, and take it to the chief steward." So they took it.

Jesus' response to his mother may have been John's way of reminding us that there is only One who can decide when it is time for the Divine to be revealed to others. Mary seemed sure that the time had come and that God was ready to do so.

The very next thing Mary did was to say to the servants, "Do whatever he tells you." There was no arguing from that point forward. We have no way of knowing what she or anyone expected to happen after that command, but her utterance of it is important.

Why do you think John included this story when it is not found elsewhere in scripture?

Think about the possible importance in these first few sentences of this part of our passage. What symbolism do you see?

Jesus was her son, to whom she looked for help, she was certain that he was also much more. For John, "to believe in Jesus as the Christ is to live a life within a life. Nothing is changed but everything is changed" (Sloyan 37). Mary recognized the true nature of Jesus: fully human and fully divine. She also set the stage for the sign to be performed and then she got out of the way and let him do what only he could do.

Jesus told the workers to take the stone jars and fill them with water. They did as they were told. In John's Gospel, "the essence of being a disciple is doing whatever Jesus commands" (Sloyan 34).

Many preachers and teachers have spent hours explaining the ways in which this story is about Jesus ending the strict purification rites of the Jewish religious elite. The stone jars would have been used for cleaning, not wine. Because of this, one could see how a person would make this the main point of the story. Jesus used what should have been kept pure to offer an abundance of wine for the party, keeping the groom from becoming an outcast and the family from being embarrassed. In truth, the story is more about the obedience of the workers and the amount of wine that Jesus produced. Jesus set the stage for the party to continue for a long time.

Scenic Route

Read John 2:9-11.

When the steward tasted the water that had become wine, and did not know where it came from (though the servants who had drawn the water knew), the steward called the bridegroom [10] and said to him, "Everyone serves the good wine first, and then the inferior wine after the guests have become drunk. But you have kept the good wine until now." [11] Jesus did this, the first of his signs, in Cana of Galilee, and revealed his glory; and his disciples believed in him.

Most Protestants move quickly past Mary's stage-setting, but it is important to pause long enough to see that "the show" would not have happened without her work.

Another important character in this tale is the steward. Stewards are found throughout scripture. Often, the steward was put in charge of all the master's affairs. Jesus told the workers to take a bit of the water (which had become wine) to the "man in charge." He would have been overseeing all of the details of the wedding party.

Surprised, the steward went to the groom and shared his shock. Traditionally, his statement "Everyone serves the good wine first, and then the inferior wine after the guests have become drunk. But you have kept the good wine until now," has been seen as a compliment, but the text does not identify it as such.

Mary saw something that Jesus did not. She pushed him to accept his call to perform this sign. When has someone pushed you beyond your comfort zone? When have you answered a calling because someone could see something in you before you were able to see it yourself? When have you done the same for someone else?

How do you react when control is taken from you when you feel that you should be in charge?

How do you feel about the steward's comment to the groom? When has something seemed like a compliment when it really wasn't?

The final statement of our passage calls the event "the first of his signs." For a first sign, this one seems odd. Not many people would have known what happened. We can assume Jesus' mother was aware. We are told that the disciples knew and believed. Other than those who were closest to Jesus, the only other characters who knew that he changed water into wine were the servants who had filled the jars.

If the sign was the important moment in that story, perhaps it is because Jesus had chosen his first disciples just before this event. This sign allowed them to see exactly whom they were following. Maybe the first sign wasn't to help out the groom. Maybe it was to help the first disciples begin their own ministry as they followed Jesus.

The sign wasn't really about Jesus changing water into wine, but about the abundance with which he did so. The six stone jars would have held about 100 gallons. No matter how great a party it was, there was no need for such excess! However, the true sign of Jesus in this strange story is that Jesus provided an abundance, both in the amount of wine as well as in the quality. This first sign points the reader to the abundance of love found in Jesus, the Christ. That is the true sign. That is the stage being set for the abundant love of Christ seen through the life, death, and resurrection of Jesus.

Workers Ahead

Our lesson presumes there is joy in setting the stage for others. In the scripture we especially see the ways in which Mary set the stage for Jesus. Our society has made setting the stage and getting out of the way more and more difficult. Our culture does not reward being in the background. We do not recognize the importance of quietly whispering to Jesus, "Do something." We are more fascinated with the deed he has done.

People have always been drawn to the performer, whether it was on stage, in the church, or elsewhere. Wait a minute, did I say "in the church"? By all means! Think for a moment about the antics in which some ministers engage in order to draw a larger crowd. Consider the approach to ministry that many television evangelists employ. I've even heard people refer to worship in some churches as being a production, entertainment.

However, we need both performers and stage-setters. Without the performer, there is no need to set the stage. And, without someone quietly moving furniture, the performer could not continue.

As you continue with your life, make a point to notice when you are the performer and when you are the stage setter. Seek ways to set the stage for others. For instance, look for ways to support a co-worker that will enable him or her to succeed.

How have the stories of Jesus helped you to follow your calling? How do they help you to understand Jesus better?

In what ways does your community of faith express the abundant love of Jesus Christ? How effective are you at doing so? How can you improve?

Do you find yourself to be more of the performer or the stage-setter? We each likely have some characteristics of both, depending on the circumstances in which we find ourselves.

Who sets the stage for you? How has that person helped you to be more faithful? more successful?

In the Rear View

When do you experience joy? What things contribute to or detract from your ability to experience joy?

The wedding in Cana was a joyous occasion on many levels. The bride and groom and their families and friends had been celebrating for a time, which we know because the wine ran out. These celebrations often lasted up to a week. Weddings were and are joyous occasions.

Mary experienced joy when Jesus intervened in a situation that would have brought shame on the groom and his family. She was present when he performed the first of many signs and wonders. It brings joy to a mother when she witnesses her child succeed.

The steward was joyful when he approached his master with the news that they had exceptionally good wine to serve to their guests. The servants were probably joyful because they didn't have to tell the steward that the supply of wine was exhausted.

I don't know whether or not Jesus and his newly chosen disciples experienced joy as a result of this experience. Jesus may have had joy because his ministry had begun and the disciples may have known joy at having agreed to follow this rabbi who could work such miracles. Regardless, we know joy because of Christ's abundant love.

Day 1:

Find a place where you can go to be quiet, where you won't be disturbed or distracted. Take this book and a pen with you. Read John 2:1-11 slowly. Sit silently as you listen for God to reveal to you a word or phrase from the scripture. If a word or phrase doesn't come to you, read the scripture again. Breathe deeply and in rhythm as you simply sit in the presence of God, repeating the word or phrase. After approximately 5 minutes, write about your experience. Reflect on what surprised you.

Day 2:

There is probably someone in your life for whom you are being called to "set the stage." In this instance, think of setting the stage as enabling someone to live into his or her true calling. In what ways are you to whisper into his or her ear, "It is time"? Spend time today thinking about this.

Find some crayons, markers, or colored pencils. Write this person's name in the area below. Begin to pray for that person while you doodle on the page. This form of prayer is called "Praying in Color," which was introduced by Sybil MacBeth. Take your time. Draw shapes, lines, or words as you focus on asking God to guide this person in his or her calling and to guide you in the role you will play in setting the stage.

Day 3:

For John, being a disciple meant doing whatever Jesus commanded. In our passage this week, we witness the servants obeying his command to fill the stone jars. If only it was so clear for each of us! Meditate today on what Christ is commanding you to do in, with, and through your life. Open yourself for the Christ to command you. Record your thoughts below.

Day 4:

All of the lessons in this unit of study are about joy. Think about those things that bring you joy. Write a prayer in which you thank God for the joy in your life.

Day 5:

List individuals and groups of people who need to find joy in their lives. Make a second list of ways that you can be instrumental in helping to bring that joy. For instance, someone who is unable to leave his or her home might experience joy through a friendly visit.

Day 6:

The first sign Jesus performed in John's Gospel is evidence of Christ's abundant love. Reflect on the ways in which you have experienced this abundant love. Journal your thoughts in the space provided.

Day 7:

 Read John 2:1-11. Now read it a second time more slowly. Breathe deeply and take in every word as you read the passage. Write down images, words, or phrases that jump out at you and reflect on what they mean for your life. Rest as you know that in God there is great joy.

Works Cited:

Sloyan, Gerard. "John 2:1-12" *John: Interpretation: A Bible Commentary for Teaching and Preaching.* Louisville: John Knox, 1988. 30-39. Print.

Joy in Being Known

Scripture for lesson:
John 4:3-26, 39-42

Written by Tiffany Hall McClung

One congregation I served hosted a ministry called Room in the Inn. For one night each week from November through March, the church opened its doors to homeless men, women, and children. They picked up these people who were homeless, took them to the church, prepared a hot meal for them, provided a place where they could shower, and a warm, safe place to sleep where they could sleep.

The guests were extremely grateful for the food, bed, and shower, but other things really seemed to touch their spirits. Such things as sitting at a table with one of us, being called by name, being asked, "What is your story?" were important. In these ways we became more than a mere shelter for the night. We became friends. We shared our names and our stories with one another. Our brothers and sisters who happened to be living without homes found a place where they were truly seen, heard, and known. Being truly known by another brings us all kinds of joy.

Prep for the Journey

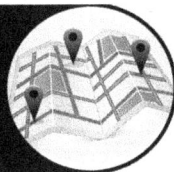

Read John 4:5-6.

So he came to a Samaritan city called Sychar, near the plot of ground that Jacob had given to his son Joseph. 6 Jacob's well was there, and Jesus, tired out by his journey, was sitting by the well. It was about noon.

I recently heard a biblical scholar preaching on this particular text. It was noted in the sermon that Jesus did not have to travel through Sychar. There were other ways around this Samaritan city. In fact, most Jewish people would have taken another road so as to avoid bumping into the Samaritans, whom the Jews despised.

The animosity between the Jews and Samaritans went back hundreds of years to the time of the divided kingdoms. Samaria was identified with the Northern Kingdom. When that kingdom fell to

How do you feel when someone remembers your name and takes the time to listen to you? What happens when this does not happen within a group?

Who are those whom we despise today? What are we willing to do to avoid them?

the Assyrians, only a remnant of the original Jewish population was left. Other peoples settled in the region and intermarriages between Jews and Gentiles began to occur. With the foreign influence, many of the people began to worship other gods. When Ezra and Nehemiah returned from captivity with groups of Jews and started to rebuild the Temple and the wall around Jerusalem, they refused to let the Samaritan Jews participate in the work.

By Jesus' time, the relationship between the two groups was extremely strained. In fact, Jews were taught at an early age that associating with someone from the opposite side was not only frowned upon, but could actually soil them and bring shame on their family.

Jesus chose to travel through a city where it was likely he would encounter someone with whom he knew he should not associate. Not only that, he traveled to the city center where it would have been impossible not meet someone. By choosing to travel into Samaria, Jesus widened the circle to include those who had not been included before. We will soon see that he knew them just as well as he did his own people.

On the Road

Jesus was resting alone at the well about noon, while his disciples went to get food, when a Samaritan woman came with a jar to get water. Jesus did the unthinkable and spoke to this woman. He simply asked her for a drink from her jar of water, which launched a serious theological debate between the two.

Read John 4:7-26.

A Samaritan woman came to draw water, and Jesus said to her, "Give me a drink." [8] (His disciples had gone to the city to buy food.)[9] The Samaritan woman said to him, "How is it that you, a Jew, ask a drink of me, a woman of Samaria?" (Jews do not share things in common with Samaritans.) [10] Jesus answered her, "If you knew the gift of God, and who it is that is saying to you, 'Give me a drink,' you would have asked him, and he would have given you living water." [11] The woman said to him, "Sir, you have no bucket, and the well is deep. Where do you get that living water? [12] Are you greater than our ancestor Jacob, who gave us the well, and with his sons and his flocks drank from it?" [13] Jesus said to her, "Everyone who drinks of this water will be thirsty again, [14] but those who drink of the water that I will give them will never be thirsty. The water that I will give will become in them a spring of water gushing up to eternal life." [15] The woman said to him, "Sir, give me this water, so that I may never be thirsty or have to keep coming here to draw water."[16] Jesus said to her, "Go, call your husband, and come back."

17 The woman answered him, "I have no husband." Jesus said to her, "You are right in saying, 'I have no husband'; 18 for you have had five husbands, and the one you have now is not your husband. What you have said is true!" 19 The woman said to him, "Sir, I see that you are a prophet. 20 Our ancestors worshiped on this mountain, but you say that the place where people must worship is in Jerusalem." 21 Jesus said to her, "Woman, believe me, the hour is coming when you will worship the Father neither on this mountain nor in Jerusalem. 22 You worship what you do not know; we worship what we know, for salvation is from the Jews. 23 But the hour is coming, and is now here, when the true worshipers will worship the Father in spirit and truth, for the Father seeks such as these to worship him. 24 God is spirit, and those who worship him must worship in spirit and truth." 25 The woman said to him, "I know that Messiah is coming" (who is called Christ). "When he comes, he will proclaim all things to us." 26 Jesus said to her, "I am he, the one who is speaking to you."

In a system of shame and honor in a world where women were viewed as subordinates to men and in which Jews and Samaritans were sworn enemies, Jesus even opening his mouth to speak to this woman was a big deal. Simply talking to her would have brought shame on himself and his family. She knew it and she called him on it. Even though he risked shame for himself, she should have given him the drink, kept her head down, and moved on. Not this woman. She was bold and strong. She basically said, "Why are you talking to me when you know you shouldn't be?"

With this question, the debate began. She knew the rules, the regulations, and the religion. When Jesus responded with a strange saying about "living water," she proved her loyalty to her own faith by invoking the name of Jacob. When he brought up the fact that she had had five husbands, she called him a prophet and tested his ability with a deeper religious question: Where is the true place of worship?

While many preachers and teachers have spent a lot of time focusing on the issue of the woman's five husbands, that is really an insignificant detail in the larger picture. Jesus made no bigger deal of it than it was. It seems to have been a way for him to prove to her that he knew what he was talking about.

When he asked the question about her husband and revealed his prophetic nature, she didn't fall down in awe of him. She leaped on the opportunity to ask the most important question—the question that points the reader to the true heart of the matter for John's text— "Where is the true place of worship?" Samaritans believed it was on the mountain. Jews believed it was in Jerusalem.

The way in which Jesus answered this question changed absolutely everything for this woman and for the world. Access to the living water does not depend on where you come from or where you worship God. In other words, the Samaritans were welcome into God's story along with the Jews and all God's children.

In what ways has the Christian Church confined its worship to particular places? One scholar called the argument between Jews and Samaritans on the proper place of worship, "the original worship wars" (Pace sermon 3/2/16). In what ways have the "worship wars" over music been a continuation of the earliest arguments of proper places of worship? Where do you find it easier to worship? What do you think about those who worship differently?

In what ways does our worship inform how we know God and others? In what ways do our relationships affect our worship?

Scenic Route

Read John 4:39-42.

Many Samaritans from that city believed in him because of the woman's testimony, "He told me everything I have ever done." ⁴⁰ So when the Samaritans came to him, they asked him to stay with them; and he stayed there two days. ⁴¹ And many more believed because of his word. ⁴² They said to the woman, "It is no longer because of what you said that we believe, for we have heard for ourselves, and we know that this is truly the Savior of the world."

In the few verses not included in our lesson, we are told that the woman left her jar and ran to tell others about her experience with the Messiah. In essence, this woman became the first evangelist. She proclaimed the good news about meeting this man who knew her inside and out. Through her proclamation, others came to know Jesus. It is no coincidence that one of the first people in the Gospel to comprehend that Jesus is the Messiah was both a woman and a Samaritan.

John's Gospel is filled with symbolism. What occurs through this story is symbolic of the healing that the Christ brings to divisions everywhere. Through this story, we see, as Gerard Sloyan writes, "An important avenue to reconciliation is acknowledging the full religious and human capacities of the 'other'" (Sloyan 59). This is the main concern of chapter four in John. We are called to know the other so that we can love the other. We are known by the Messiah and we can know others in order to share the love of the Messiah. This kind of knowing is filled with joy.

Who are the "others" in your life whom you are called to know? How will you get to know them so that you can share the Messiah's love? How would doing so bring you joy? bring joy to the other person?

Workers Ahead

Reconciliation is needed in many areas of life, even within the church. As Christians, we are called to be agents of reconciliation whenever possible. A key element to that reconciliation is knowing one another. When we know the other person's story, when we know him or her as a person, then usually we can come to an understanding. That understanding may not be agreement, but we can agree to disagree.

The Church is called to be an instrument of peace, which means helping to resolve issues that separate people. Some folks tend to think that the Church needs to stay out of such situations, but Jesus certainly didn't. As a group, identify situations that need reconcili-

When have you witnessed agreement come from two groups or two people getting to know each other? What did it take for them to develop a relationship of mutual respect?

ation. Then consider ways your faith community can be an agent of that reconciliation.

Imagine yourself as the woman at the well. As a group, write a call to worship from her point of view. In what ways would she have praised God? What can you imagine her saying to the people as she ran to tell them about Jesus? Use these words as the call to worship. Give the call to worship to your pastor or worship team and ask that it be used in worship.

In the Rear View

Jesus' discussion with the woman is evidence of the reconciliation brought to people through the love of God in the Christ. God knows us, truly knows us, and loves us. We are called to know others and love them too.

In your times of prayer and worship, allow yourself to be known by Christ. We often attempt to "put on a good face" with God as if we can hide something. The truth is that we don't want to recognize those things in ourselves, so we refuse to acknowledge them before God. Open yourself to God, who already knows you and loves you, regardless of the things you have done. Offer the same kind of acceptance to others as you get to know them. Celebrate the joy of being known by God and others!

How do you feel about the church being involved in efforts of reconciliation? What are some of the benefits and drawbacks of such actions?

How do you proclaim the good news of Jesus? If you were running to tell others about this man who knows everything about you, what would you say to them?

In what ways can you get to know someone else better? How can you let others get to know you better?

Travel Log

Day 1:

Worship often becomes something we do automatically, without really considering what we are doing or why. Reflect on the ways in which you have become complacent in worship. Journal your thoughts.

Look for opportunities to worship God in new places among new people. When you have done so, look back at your journaling and compare your feelings.

Day 2:

Fill a clear glass with water. Find a quiet place to sit and place the glass of water in front of you. Meditate on the ways in which Jesus is the "living water" in your life. When you are ready, drink the water. Feel it as it goes down your throat. Thank God for the water, for Jesus, and for the ways in which you are truly known. Write a few words about your experience in the space provided.

Day 3:

Find a bulletin from your church's worship service. If your congregation doesn't use a printed bulletin or if you don't have a copy, make a list of all the elements of worship you remember. Using the bulletin or list, reflect on the parts of worship that mean the most to you. How would you feel if those parts were changed or left out of worship? Think about the style of worship with which you are most comfortable. Try to identify why you prefer this style as opposed to others.

Day 4:

The woman at the well was not afraid to ask Jesus questions. She was bold and strong and willing to claim what she believed to be true. What questions do you have for the Christ? Write down your questions and then answer them by imagining you are the Christ. Have a conversation on paper.

Day 5:

Imagine you meet the Christ out in public the way the woman did. Mentioning her five husbands gave the woman insight to know that Jesus was a prophet. What would Jesus say to you that would cause you to realize that he knew you inside and out? After spending time on this list, thank God for God's unconditional love for you, despite knowing every detail about you.

Day 6:

Identify those people who do not have ready access to clean water. How can you provide water for one or more of these people/groups? Maybe you keep bottled water in your car to give to people you see who are living on the street. Maybe you can take a case of water to a local shelter. Maybe you can make a donation to a group such as Living Waters for the World (http://www.livingwatersfortheworld.org/) or another such organization that works to provide clean water for various areas of the world. However you choose to provide water to someone who needs it, do so in a worshipful manner, remembering that Christ is the living water.

Day 7:

Read John 4:5-26, 39-42. Read it a second time more slowly. Breathe deeply and take in every word as you read the passage. Write down images, words, or phrases that jump out at you. Reflect on those words, images, or phrases and journal your thoughts.

Works Cited:
Sloyan, Gerard. "John 4:1-54" *John: Interpretation: A Bible Commentary for Teaching and Preaching*. Louisville: John Knox, 1988. 51-60. Print.

Joy at the Heart of the Gospel

Scripture for lesson:
Luke 15:1-10

Written by Tiffany Hall McClung

In my family (and I imagine yours as well) there are stories that we tell again and again. It seems we have at least one story per family member that is pulled out and dusted off at Christmas each year. One of those stories is about my sister Tammy.

Our father was a pastor. He and my mother were chaperoning a church trip to Six Flags. Dad was driving the church bus and Mom was helping with all the kids, including her own four! On the way back to Birmingham from Atlanta, they stopped for gas and, of course, everyone filed off the bus to use the restrooms and get snacks. After filling up, Dad jumped back into the driver's seat and everyone settled in for the rest of the trip. They left—without Tammy, who was still in the restroom.

When Tammy came out, she found the gas station empty of her church group. The man behind the counter gave her a soda and assured her that her parents would soon realize what had happened and come back. This was long before cell phones, so all Tammy could do was wait. Meanwhile, my father zoomed down the interstate with his sights on home.

I don't know how long it was before Mom realized Tammy wasn't on the bus. I don't know if my mother had a moment like the mom in the movie *Home Alone* had when she realized that she had just left one of her children behind. When the story is told at the dinner table, it is done with lots of laughter, but I don't imagine there was much to laugh about in those moments. I know my mom well enough to know that she would have been absolutely terrified during the time she waited to see Tammy again. Tammy wasn't exactly lost, but there was great rejoicing when she was found. She stayed where she was because she knew those who loved her would come and get her. It is this assurance in the gospel that brings us great joy. Wherever we are, God will come and find us.

How has God found you?

Prep for the Journey

Read Luke 15:1-2.

Now all the tax collectors and sinners were coming near to listen to him. ² And the Pharisees and the scribes were grumbling and saying, "This fellow welcomes sinners and eats with them."

With two sentences, the writer of Luke says so much. Tax collectors and sinners wanted to hear what Jesus had to say. Wherever he went, they followed and listened to him. On the opposite end of things were the Pharisees and scribes. As the religious and political leaders, they should have been first in line to listen to this rabbi. Instead, they stood off to the side, grumbling and complaining because Jesus associated with tax collectors and sinners.

In the chapters leading up to this passage, Jesus had grown increasingly popular with the masses; the Pharisees' hatred of him had grown proportionately. He healed on the Sabbath; chastised dinner guests for observing cultural norms about places of honor; talked about humility and discipleship, seeming to imply that those in places of power had gotten it all wrong. He even had the audacity to claim that God would bless the lowly ones. It is no wonder the Pharisees and scribes were grumbling. By dining with tax collectors and sinners, Jesus publicly continued to protest the status quo.

It is often easy to put ourselves in the place of the sinners and tax collectors. We see ourselves as the chosen and the Pharisees as the bad guys. The truth is that the Pharisees understood and followed the Law, both religious and societal. Those of us who are active in the Church would do well to imagine that we are the Pharisees holding on to tradition and law as the Christ turns everything upside down.

Jesus used parables as a way to convey his message. The Greek word that we translate as parable literally means "that which is tossed alongside." In other words, a parable is a comparison or an analogy. A parable causes the listener to work. Jesus told these two stories to cause the Pharisees to think deeply about what truly brings God joy. Spoiler alert: It isn't following the rules!

On the Road

Read Luke 15:3-7.

So he told them this parable: ⁴ "Which one of you, having a hundred sheep and losing one of them, does not leave the ninety-nine in

What status quo is Jesus calling us to challenge today?

How does the image of Jesus turning everything upside down speak to you?

Where do you see yourself in this story? a grumbling Pharisee? a sinner pushing your way through the crowd? Imagine yourself as each of these characters. Which feels most like you? What does Jesus have to say to you?

Those listening to Jesus as he told this story would have been familiar with shepherds. Imagine Jesus telling a similar parable to your church today. What analogy might he use to share God's joy at the lost being found?

the wilderness and go after the one that is lost until he finds it? [5] *When he has found it, he lays it on his shoulders and rejoices.* [6] *And when he comes home, he calls together his friends and neighbors, saying to them, 'Rejoice with me, for I have found my sheep that was lost.'* [7] *Just so, I tell you, there will be more joy in heaven over one sinner who repents than over ninety-nine righteous persons who need no repentance.*

The Pharisees were standing nearby as Jesus told this parable. They thought they had it all figured out. After all, they were religious professionals who took great pride in following the exactness of the Law. They had even taught others to follow the Law of Moses. So, it makes sense that they were confused. When they found Jesus, who was a rabbi (teacher), dining with tax collectors and sinners, they didn't understand how a teacher could live so far outside the law.

We do not know why Jesus singled out tax collectors, but we do know that they were hated because they worked for the Roman government, which ruled the Jewish territory. For Jesus to have welcomed them would have been seen as an affront to his own race as well as his religion. In other words, by all standards at the time, Jesus was the one doing wrong.

In response to the Pharisees' grumbling, Jesus told a story about a lost sheep. His audience would have been familiar with the role of a shepherd. However, they would have viewed this shepherd as being wealthy because he had a flock of one hundred sheep. Many shepherds maintained flocks of only twenty or so sheep. We can assume that Jesus' use of a larger number was to drive home the fact that the shepherd could have easily lived without the one sheep. He could have chosen to write it off as a loss on the books and taken the ninety-nine home for the night. Jesus assumed in the telling, though, that any of the listeners would have understood going to find the one sheep. Even though it was one of one hundred, it would have been worth something.

Like many of Jesus' stories, this one has an economic component. Again, we don't know, but it is possible that Jesus was appealing to the greed of those in the crowd. He asked, "Who wouldn't leave the ninety-nine to go find the one that would bring in cash through its wool?" Those listening would have found the lost sheep and rejoiced. The crowd was with him so far. Then he turned the tables on them.

Just when he had them understanding how joyous they would feel if they found a lost sheep, Jesus surprised them by saying that God is more joyous than that when sinners are found. The Pharisees had asked why Jesus associated with sinners and tax collectors. Jesus responded by telling them that God loves them and rejoices when they come to Christ. Fred Craddock says that this "joy is the heart of the gospel" (186).

Read Luke 15:8-10.

"Or what woman having ten silver coins, if she loses one of them, does not light a lamp, sweep the house, and search carefully until she finds it? [9] *When she has found it, she calls together her friends and neighbors, saying, 'Rejoice with me, for I have found the coin that I had lost.'* [10] *Just so, I tell you, there is joy in the presence of the angels of God over one sinner who repents."*

In Luke's Gospel, inclusion is a constant. Having told a story that would have resonated with the men in the crowd, Jesus told a second story that would have appealed to the women. His inclusion of both men and women was important as he shared God's joy in finding the lost. There is a place for everyone in God's kingdom.

The woman in the second parable was probably a peasant, which means that the coins likely were *denarii*—each equivalent to a day's labor. That money would have fed the woman's family for about three days. Losing one of the coins meant the difference between her family being able to eat adequately one day but not the next. No wonder she searched so diligently for the lost coin!

The parable tells us that God searches for "sinners" in the same way. *Sinner* in that world wasn't automatically one who was known for moral failures. At that time, sin was anything that made one unworthy of God or the people of God. So, being unable to pay your Temple tax, practicing a despised occupation, being born illegitimately, etc., made a person a sinner in that world. That's why tax collectors and sinners are so closely linked in the New Testament.

In response to the Pharisees' questions of how Jesus can welcome sinners and tax collectors, Jesus told these two stories. Each one ends with such joy that a party is thrown. Both the man and the woman call together their friends and neighbors and share the joy of finding what had been lost. "The joy is so abundant that it cannot be contained; one person alone cannot adequately celebrate it; there must be a party to which others are invited" (Craddock 185-186).

The Pharisees wanted to know why Jesus hung out with known sinners. He did so because he understood what joy God experiences when even one sinner repents and is restored to a relationship with God.

Certain occupations were despised because the people who worked in them couldn't keep the purity rules, i.e. fishermen, tanners, shepherds, tax collectors, etc. A man was born into an occupation, doing what his father did.

Reflect on a time in your life when you found something that was lost. How did you feel? How did you celebrate?

Workers Ahead

Finding and restoring what had been lost was very important to the Christ. According to these parables, it was much more important than obeying the Jewish laws.

You probably know people who are "lost," people who do not have a relationship with God. We are to seek out such individuals and share with them the joy of a life lived with God.

As a group, reflect on the ways in which you can be more welcoming to all people. List the ways in which you already welcome them. Imagine ways you can reach out further. Start by forming relationships, getting to know people. Remember a previous lesson about the joy of being known? Some of those same principles apply here. Jesus seems to have invited folks to hang out with him, to have a meal with him. Simply being present and available is key.

Plan a celebration of God's love and acceptance. Take this celebration to people who do not have a relationship with God. Let them see the joy that can be found in that relationship. Your attitude as you interact with people will speak volumes, so be positive and let your joy shine through your actions.

In the Rear View

The joy at the heart of the gospel is finding and restoring what is lost. Jesus understood this, so he welcomed everyone to follow him. He dined with sinners in order to share the good news of God. The good news is that God longs to be in relationship with each and every person. A party occurs in heaven every time a person accepts that relationship.

The Pharisees knew the scriptures and the rules, which they thought everyone should follow as closely as they did. It must have been difficult for them to hear Jesus tell these two stories, realizing that he was setting them against the sinners who were welcomed into God's kingdom. In the first parable, Jesus even said that one sinner restored is better than ninety-nine righteous. Presumably, the Pharisees would have seen themselves as the righteous. Jesus was not subtle. In addition, he was so certain of his point that he made it multiple times!

With each of the parables, there is an economic factor. Both the sheep and the coin would have meant at least a day's wages for the one who had lost them. Jesus often included economics in his teach-

Where in your own community could you imagine Jesus gathering with the sinners and tax collectors of today? Who would the Pharisees of today be?

As a person in the church, what would be difficult for you to hear Jesus say? Why?

ings. It is not farfetched to imagine that a tax collector would have chosen that profession as a last resort, and certainly others among them would have struggled financially. They truly listened to Jesus and would have understood how important it was to find what was lost. They would have known the joy of which Jesus spoke in the finding. They would also have been able to imagine the joy that God feels at finding each person who is "lost."

Day 1:

Think about being a sheep. A lost sheep is vulnerable. Without the herd, the sheep is more likely to be attacked by a predator, to be cold, to get hurt, etc. In other words, it is risky to be a lost sheep. Journal your responses, thinking especially about how God cares for the sheep that are lost.

Day 2:

Take pens, crayons, markers, colored pencils and this book to a quiet place. Think of someone you consider to be "lost," remembering that there are many ways in which someone can be lost. Write this person's name in the center of the space below. Begin to pray for that person while you doodle on the page with your crayons/markers/colored pencils.

Day 3:

Take this book and your Bible to a quiet place that is free of distractions. As you read Luke 15:1-10, imagine yourself as one of the sinners in the crowd to whom Jesus was speaking. Write as if you are journaling about your experience after hearing Jesus say these things. Be as specific as you can while pretending you were in the crowd that day. Then imagine yourself as one of the Pharisees and do the same thing.

Day 4:

Reflect on the ways in which you feel lost. Spend quiet time in prayer about these things. Journal about your feelings. Ask God to help you feel found. Know that God is filled with joy when you are!

Day 5:

Take a walk today. Look for a "found object." Find something that reminds you of the joy that God has in you. Choose something that you can pick up and take with you, such as a leaf, rock, or a piece of litter. Hold it and imagine the party that God has thrown in heaven because God loves you so much. Take the object with you and put it where you will be reminded daily to thank God for God's joy in you. Write a prayer of thanks for God's love and joy.

Day 6:

Using the space provided, complete the following sentence stem: "There will be more joy in heaven…" Just write; do not edit yourself or cross out. If you get stuck, go back to the prompt and write it again and again until something else comes to your mind. When approximately five minutes have passed, read out loud what you have written. Reflect on surprises or things you learned about the passage from this exercise.

Day 7:
You may find that your relationship with God it isn't bringing you or God much joy these days. Make some notes about the things that seem to be interfering with the joy. Offer a prayer of confession, being honest with yourself and with God.

Works Cited:
Craddock, Fred. "The Parable of the Sower (8:4-18) (Matthew 13:1-23; Mark 4:1-25)" *Luke: Interpretation: A Bible Commentary for Teaching and Preaching*. Louisville: John Knox, 1990. 107-110. Print.

Craddock, Fred. "Luke 15:1-32: Three Parables of Joy" *Luke: Interpretation: A Bible Commentary for Teaching and Preaching*. Louisville: John Knox, 1990. 183-186. Print.

Joy in Thanksgiving

Scripture for lesson:
Luke 17:11-19

Written by Tiffany Hall McClung

How likely are you to give thanks for the joys you experience in life?

When I was about seven months pregnant with our first child, my mid-wife discovered something was wrong. She sent me to a doctor who specialized in high-risk pregnancies. You can imagine how terrifying it was to be told I was in the midst of a high-risk pregnancy. The amniotic fluid was decreasing and they could do nothing other than monitor the situation. We were told that labor would likely have to be induced when the fluid was too low to sustain the baby. Then, I was told to live life normally—other than the two doctor visits per week.

At one particular visit to the doctor, during the ultrasound to check the fluid levels, the doctor asked, "Are you ready to go have a baby today?" Of course we weren't! We should have had about six more weeks to get ready, but it was safer for our baby boy to have labor induced than for him to remain in the womb. As soon as he was born, a nurse rushed him to the nursery for monitoring. Not long after that, he had to be moved to the Neonatal Intensive Care Unit (NICU). When they finally let us visit him, he was covered in tubes and had an IV in his scalp.

Barbara, a nurse, introduced herself to us, explaining that she would be our son's nurse while he was in the NICU. We were very lucky as our son spent only a week in the NICU. Many babies spend months there.

Looking back, I know how lucky we were. At the time, though, it was the scariest thing I had ever experienced. I didn't know what was going on or what to expect. I wondered if he would survive, if we would ever take him home to the room that had been prepared just for him. Without Barbara's love and concern that week, we would have been inconsolable. With her patience, kindness, and care for our son, Barbara offered healing to us.

Around our son's first birthday, we took a picture of him—healthy as could be—and mailed it to Barbara so that she could add his picture to the many others who had survived the NICU. We thanked her for her love and care and assured her that she had provided all manner of healing in our lives. We felt deep gratitude for what she had done for us and for our baby. We wanted to share that thanksgiving with her. There is joy in thanksgiving.

Prep for the Journey

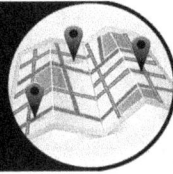

Read Luke 17:11-13.

On the way to Jerusalem Jesus was going through the region between Samaria and Galilee. ¹² As he entered a village, ten lepers approached him. Keeping their distance, ¹³ they called out, saying, "Jesus, Master, have mercy on us!"

By this point in Luke's Gospel, Jesus had said many radical things. It seems that everywhere he went, religious leaders were waiting in the shadows, hoping to hear him say something for which they could pounce on him. So, it is no surprise that this particular passage begins with the reminder of where Jesus was going. "On the way to Jerusalem" was Luke's way of reminding the reader that Jesus was already on the journey to the cross. With every teaching and healing, Jesus continued to seal his fate.

While the leaders with all the power saw a troublemaker with whom they must deal, those who were outcasts saw Jesus clearly. As he made the journey to Jerusalem, ten lepers approached him, calling him Master. For Luke, this way of addressing Jesus showed the authority with which Jesus acted. The other synoptic Gospels use teacher or rabbi, which connote important aspects of the ministry of the Christ. Luke put the word *master* in the mouths of the lepers to reiterate Jesus' power and authority.

Jesus was traveling between Samaria and Galilee. We will see in later verses that the one leper who returned to thank Jesus was a Samaritan. We assume that the others were Jewish, which seems probable since the writer found it important to mention that the returning leper was Samaritan. From other stories in the Gospels, we know that Samaritans and Jews were enemies.

Lepers created their own colonies. In a world that focused on purity laws and maintaining boundaries between Samaritans and Jews, once a person developed leprosy his or her views of the world changed. Because lepers were cast out of their own communities, they had to find another community in which to live. The boundaries between Jew and Samaritan were wiped away by mutual illness. They created their own colonies, and all lepers were welcome regardless of birthplace.

In addition, we know that lepers were required by law to keep a certain distance from those who did not have the disease. Had they not kept their distance, they would have been breaking the law. The third thing we know from other scriptures about lepers is that their colonies were located along well-trafficked areas. Because of their illness, they would not have had the opportunity to work. Pan-handling was their only source of income. Jesus passed by such a place and found himself being asked to show mercy on these lepers.

Why do you think Jesus didn't "cool it" for a while so that his earthly ministry could have lasted longer?

What is the significance of the word *master* in this scripture? Often in our own culture, this word brings negative feelings. How do you feel about using this word for Jesus? Do you ever use it in your personal prayers? If so, what does it mean to you? If not, what other words do you use that express the authority of the Christ?

Who are the lepers of today? How do you react when one of them calls out to you?

On the Road

What blessings do you take for granted? How will you change your attitude?

What does it mean to go and show one's self to the priest?

What symbolism do you see in this story of the ten lepers?

What symbols do we use in our everyday lives to keep us filled with gratitude to God for healing in Christ?

Read Luke 17:14-16.

When he saw them, he said to them, "Go and show yourselves to the priests." And as they went, they were made clean. ¹⁵ Then one of them, when he saw that he was healed, turned back, praising God with a loud voice. ¹⁶ He prostrated himself at Jesus' feet and thanked him. And he was a Samaritan.

A scholar writing in an article published at BibleGateway.com says, "Those who do not take blessings for granted make up an exclusive club of surprising people." The ten lepers did not even have to make it all the way to the priests before there was evidence of healing. The Gospel writer puts it this way, "And as they went…" In their going, on their way, walking along, regardless of the way in which it is translated, it is clear that the healing took place quickly and without the aid of any others. The ritual of having the priest look at them was not to aid in the healing, but to allow them to return to the community. A religious leader who had been trained to do so would have to examine those who claimed to be healed. If they approved, the healed person could resume a normal life. To be welcomed would have been a very big deal for persons who had been shunned for so long.

Some scholars speculate that the Samaritan was not in need of the Jewish priest's approval, which is why he returned to thank Jesus. It is more likely that the writer of Luke was making a point. Jesus' healing is open to all who will receive it, both Samaritans and Jews. Just in case there were Jews in the audience who still wanted to keep Samaritans on the outside, making the Samaritan the hero of the story drove home the point that God's love extends to all and welcomes everyone.

Luke often used the Hebrew Scriptures as inspiration. He took pleasure in modeling the stories of Jesus after ancient texts. For example, there are similarities between this story of the healing of the grateful leper and 2 Kings 5:10-15 where Naaman was healed of leprosy by following Elisha's instructions. The main point of Naaman's healing is that it was his conversion to Israel's faith, which is also an important factor in Luke's telling. The verb used in verse 19 that translates as "made well" can also be translated as "to be saved."

Scenic Route

Read Luke 17:17-19.

Then Jesus asked, "Were not ten made clean? But the other nine, where are they? [18] Was none of them found to return and give praise to God except this foreigner?" [19] Then he said to him, "Get up and go on your way; your faith has made you well."

If the reader chooses to think of "your faith has made you well" as "your faith has caused you to be saved," how does this change the reading, if at all? Fred Craddock believes it does. He writes that the story of the ten lepers has two parts. The first is the story we see on the surface. It is a story of healing much like many other stories of healing throughout the Bible.

Craddock claims there is a second part, though, which is about the salvation of a foreigner. As such, it would have held much significance for the readers of Luke. As noted above, it was important for Luke that readers understand that the Samaritans were welcomed into the Kingdom of God just like the Jews. In addition, he used moments like the Samaritan's return to give thanks for the healing as a way to encourage new ways of seeing "the enemy" that had been kept at a distance for far too long.

Jesus had already healed the Samaritan, so why would he need to say, "Your faith has made you well"? We do not believe that the other lepers found their healing to be short-lived because they did not also return. Something much more eternal was at work in Jesus' statement. He was welcoming the foreigner into the Kingdom and providing evidence to all who would hear that God welcomes everyone who will accept the invitation.

Workers Ahead

When Jesus healed the lepers, he had already been creating problems for those who upheld the status quo. Jesus associating with the Samaritan leper would have been scandalous enough, but he took it even further by calling attention to the goodness in the Samaritan. What Jesus really did was far more scandalous: He welcomed the Samaritan into God's Kingdom, treated him as a chosen one of God, and praised his faith.

In telling the healed Samaritan, "Your faith has made you well," Jesus was really saying, "Your faith has saved you." There is no indica-

---

What is the significance that only one of the ten lepers returned to thank Jesus?

In what ways has God provided you with new ways to see "the enemy"? How has God enabled you to see your enemies as children of God?

Whom does society shun? How does the Church contribute to the shunning? How can the Church follow Jesus' example and welcome all people?

tion that the Samaritan expected this reaction. All we are told in the text is that the Samaritan returned to praise God with a loud voice, lie at Jesus' feet, and thank him for what he had done.

Jesus' statement leads one to wonder about connections between thanksgiving, joy, and salvation. Discuss these possible connections either as a total group or in groups of three-five people. After about 15 minutes, have each small group share its reflections with the larger group. Make a list of the connections between thanksgiving, joy, and salvation. Offer a prayer thanking God for each of those things.

Jesus always welcomed those whom society felt were undesirable, which he did again with the Samaritan. Those in power would have accepted this incident as yet more evidence that Jesus defied all of their cultural norms. Rather than seeing it for the beautiful moment of redemption and inclusion that it was, they added it to their growing list of reasons to get rid of Jesus.

Most people would agree that we need to be accepting of all people, but interacting with them may be another story. Would you invite a former inmate to your home? a homeless person? Why or why not? How would you feel if a former addict or prostitute joined your church? How likely would you be to sit beside him or her? How do you treat people who are from the Middle East? Why?

Plan an activity that will put you in close contact with groups of people who are often shunned, that will take you outside your comfort zone. A variety of activities come to mind including joint worship services, providing meals to people who are homeless, visiting those who are imprisoned, etc. After the activity, get together as a group and talk about the experience.

In the Rear View

Much joy comes to us through true thanksgiving. In the scripture passage for this lesson, we witnessed the gratitude of the Samaritan who returned to lay at Jesus' feet and praise God loudly for the healing he had received. We can't help but wonder about the other nine lepers. Jesus certainly did. Why did they not return? Was it because they took for granted the healing that Jesus had provided to them? Too often we take for granted the good things in our lives, things that come from others as well as from God.

With the Samaritan as your example of joyous gratitude, spend time this week expressing true thanksgiving. Each day make a list of things for which you are grateful. However, don't limit your thanksgiving to a written list. Find ways to express joyful thanksgiving to others. Notice when the words "Thank you" become rote or meaningless and work to change your attitude. When you thank someone, look the person in the eye and be specific with your expression of gratitude.

Thank others for the true healing beneath the surface. Someone may offer you a cup of coffee for which you would ordinarily simply say, "Thanks." The coffee is offered, though, at a moment when it reminds you of your deceased parent or lifts your spirits on a really hard day. Take time to thank the person for being kind in a world that needs it. You don't have to share every detail of your life. Simply be more specific with your thanksgiving. Take time to accept thanksgiving as well. When others thank you, don't dismiss it as we too often do by saying, "Oh, it's nothing." Instead, receive the gratitude and return it to the other person. "You are so welcome" or "It means a lot to me to be able to do this for you" can be important for another person to hear. Practice joyful thanksgiving.

Travel Log

Day 1:

Think about those people whom your group identified as being shunned by society. What can you do individually to let these people experience the healing available through the Christ? Make some notes and then take action.

Day 2:

Read Luke 17:11-19 and imagine yourself as the leper who returned to thank Jesus. Then write as if you are journaling about your experience after being in the presence of the Messiah. Be as specific as you can while pretending you are the leper. Take time to read what you have written when you are finished.

Day 3:

After reading Luke 17:11-19, imagine yourself as one of the lepers who did not return to thank Jesus. Then write as if you are journaling about your experience after being made well. Be as specific as you can while pretending you are one of the lepers. Take time to read what you have written when you are finished.

Day 4:

Write an actual paper thank you note to someone. Be specific as you share your gratitude with this person. Mail the note to the person when it is complete.

Day 5:

Recall any recent experiences of practicing joyful thanksgiving—either as a recipient or a giver. Journal about the difference your attitude made in how you experienced those times.

Day 6:

Write using this prompt, "Your faith has made you well…" Do not edit yourself or cross out. If you get stuck and feel like nothing is coming to you, go back to the prompt and write it again and again until something else comes to your mind. After five minutes or so, read aloud what you wrote. Reflect on surprises or things you learned about the passage from this time.

Day 7:
Everyone experiences a sense of salvation differently. You may have had a "lightning bolt moment," or you may have been formed through time in a life lived in the church. Regardless of your experience of understanding salvation in your own life, reflect on your gratitude for that salvation. Imagine yourself returning to the Christ to thank him for healing you. Write some things you might do or say to the Christ.

Works Cited:
"BibleGateway.com:" A Searchable Online Bible in over 100 Versions and 50 Languages. IVP NT Commentary Series. N.p., 3.24.16. Web.

Craddock, Fred. "Teachings Leading to the Final Prediction of the Passion" *Luke: Interpretation: A Bible Commentary for Teaching and Preaching.* Louisville: John Knox, 1990. 201-204. Print.

Joy in the Midst of Grief

Scripture for lesson:
John 12:1-8

Written by Tiffany Hall McClung

The day my father was diagnosed with terminal cancer was one of the most joyous days I've experienced. I realize how crazy that sounds. I don't have time or space to give too many of the details, but because of some very strange circumstances, all six members of my family were together when the doctor delivered the news. My three siblings and I stood around Dad and Mom. We all knew it was coming, and we wanted to be together when we heard it out loud. Dad, as he was known to do, quickly made a joke, which caused us all to burst into laughter through our tears.

The rest of the day was spent just like that: Lots of tears and lots of laughter. We spent some of the best hours my family had had together, gathered around the table as my mom served us tea and chocolate pie. The way in which there can be such joy in the midst of terrible anguish and grief is mysterious.

Prep for the Journey

Read John 12:1-2.

Six days before the Passover Jesus came to Bethany, the home of Lazarus, whom he had raised from the dead. ² There they gave a dinner for him. Martha served, and Lazarus was one of those at the table with him.

What seems like an insignificant detail, "the home of Lazarus, whom he had raised from the dead," was quite important. In the previous chapter, Jesus had arrived at the home of his friends, Mary, Martha, and Lazarus after Lazarus had already been dead for a few days. Martha ran to Jesus before he could even get to the house, saying that IF he had been there, her brother would not be dead. She also demonstrated great faith by proclaiming that "even now I know that God will give you whatever you ask of him" (John 11:22). Jesus replied, "Your brother will rise again," and he proceeded to bring Lazarus back to life.

How do you handle grief?

What details in your faith journey might seem insignificant to someone else? Why are they important to you?

In John's Gospel, this act seems to have been the last straw for the religious leaders. In response to the resurrection of Lazarus, they began to plot Jesus' demise. The leaders were watching and waiting for Jesus to show up so that they could arrest him. They also wanted Lazarus out of the way because his resurrection from the dead had caused many people to believe in Jesus.

Everyone at this dinner would have been breaking the law because they were entertaining not one, but two fugitives. One can imagine that the party was filled with a certain tension as they all began to realize that the religious and political leaders were not going to give up until they had Jesus and Lazarus in custody. This dinner was the first time Jesus had ventured close to Jerusalem since raising Lazarus from the dead. As people began to arrive in Jerusalem to celebrate the Passover, the authorities put check-points in place throughout the city in hopes of spotting Jesus so that they could arrest him.

On the Road

Read John 12:3-6.

Mary took a pound of costly perfume made of pure nard, anointed Jesus' feet, and wiped them with her hair. The house was filled with the fragrance of the perfume. ⁴ But Judas Iscariot, one of his disciples (the one who was about to betray him), said, ⁵ "Why was this perfume not sold for three hundred denarii and the money given to the poor?" ⁶ (He said this not because he cared about the poor, but because he was a thief; he kept the common purse and used to steal what was put into it.)

In the midst of this dinner, Mary stepped up and did something completely out of the normal realm. It was extravagant and sensual, scandalous and beautiful. It was her way of showing that she knew Jesus, really knew him, and understood where that week would lead him.

In the same way that the woman at the well was the first in John's Gospel to understand that Jesus was the Messiah, Mary was the first to understand what being the Messiah meant. At a dinner with her brother, Lazarus, whom Jesus had raised from the dead, Mary dared to enter the group of men. She knew that Jesus was going to die, so she anointed him.

Mary is an unusual character in this scene around the table. She shouldn't have been there. She should have been helping Martha serve the meal. Of course, there is nothing in this text that suggests she hadn't been serving, but we know from the larger context that Mary was a disciple—not one of the twelve, but a disciple nonetheless. Her action proves her place among his followers.

Mary humbled herself before Jesus and anointed him with per-

How does it feel to think of Jesus as being a fugitive? In what circumstances might you entertain a fugitive?

113

Why do you think the writer of John chose to include the parenthetical statements about the true motives of Judas? Read the scripture again but leave those out. If they had never been there, how would that have changed the way people have read and understood this scripture over the years?

fume that was to be used at the time of a burial. Even though it cost an entire year's wages, Mary poured the fragrance over Jesus' feet and wiped them with her hair. In this place of humility, she bowed to the Christ, the Messiah, who had started his journey toward the cross. In John's Gospel, Jesus was anointed before he entered Jerusalem. In some way, Mary was preparing him for what was about to occur.

The reader knows the cost of the perfume because John put those words in the mouth of Judas. John also let the reader know that Judas' objection to the expense was not due to care and concern for the poor. Judas was a thief, having stolen from the funds given for the group's use. Without this parenthetical statement, it would have seemed a perfectly reasonable question. Why would Mary seemingly waste such expensive perfume on Jesus, who was alive and well? Only she seemed to understand what was coming. There must have been joy in the midst of that grief, joy in truly knowing the Christ, joy in being able to share that sacred moment with him before his body was beaten and destroyed. We do not know how much she understood, but it is safe to assume that she understood something was coming. Her act was one of lavish love, given as a way to prepare Jesus for what was coming.

Scenic Route

Read John 12:7-8.

Jesus said, "Leave her alone. She bought it so that she might keep it for the day of my burial. ⁸ You always have the poor with you, but you do not always have me."

Jesus' response to Judas makes it clear that he appreciated and understood Mary's act, which was scandalous for several reasons: As a woman, she should not have approached a man without him speaking to her first. Second, she touched him! Imagine how scandalous it was for her to wipe his feet with her hair, which should not have been loose! And, third, she was anointing someone in a manner that was done in preparation for burial. Jesus was alive, sitting among his closest friends when she began to anoint him, touch him, and speak to him.

Because Jesus knew Mary's heart, he understood her actions. When Judas attempted to put her in her place, Jesus stood up for her. What he said has been the source of all kinds of trouble throughout the years.

First, he announced his own burial, which must have shaken the disciples as they appeared to be clueless for much of the time. Then, he said, "You always have the poor with you…" This phrase has been used again and again to justify the Christian Church's focus on making disciples rather than caring for God's people. The problem is that one can't be a true disciple without also caring for God's people. Without following Jesus' commands to feed, clothe, and visit the least of these, we aren't being very good disciples.

Jesus was not the first to say "You always have the poor." In fact, he was quoting from the Law in Deuteronomy, chapter fifteen, that says, "Since there will never cease to be some in need on the earth, I therefore command you, 'Open your hand to the poor and needy neighbor in your land.'" This command comes in the midst of an entire chapter on the canceling of debts every seventh year.

In other words, Jesus responded to Judas with the Law. We know from John's asides that Judas had evil motives. He attempted to ridicule Mary's action by bringing the poor into the situation, to which Jesus responded, "Right! There are lots of people who are poor, so go take care of them!" Jesus' intent was not that the needs of people who are poor be pushed aside, but that Mary be allowed to express her grief any way she desired and that they should take care of the poor. Jesus knew that Judas was more concerned with embarrassing Mary for stepping out of bounds than he was with truly helping those in need. So, Jesus put him in his place by quoting the law, with which Judas would have been very familiar.

Workers Ahead

Sometimes God calls us to break free of the constraints put on us by others. Mary risked bringing shame on herself and her family because she dared to step out of her place. Societal rules were so important that Mary may have been shunned when others heard what she had dared to do—and for a known fugitive!

Mary's gift was extravagant in terms of its monetary cost, but it was also a gift of extravagant love. In what way can you share an extravagant gift with someone who needs it? Don't feel like you have to spend a year's wages on it! Extravagance can take many different forms. It could be as simple as buying a meal for the homeless person in the parking lot, volunteering to babysit for the single mother, or visiting someone who is lonely. It could be as extravagant as planning a get-away weekend for someone can't afford it or who has been under a lot of stress. Don't do something that is going to feel like a burden, though.

Mary willingly humbled herself, offering her actions as a gift of love to Jesus. While Jesus is not physically present among us, we can find Jesus in many others, including those who may be sick, in prison, hungry, etc. Consider as a group some ways you can offer yourselves as a gift of love in Christ's name. Maybe it is time you cleaned out

How do you feel about caring for those who are poor? Why? How effective are your church's current ministries in caring for those who are poor? What needs to be added or changed?

How might God be calling you to "step out of place"? What might you be risking to do so? How willing are you to take that risk?

What loving action can you take that shares extravagant faith?

In what ways should you humble yourself? How can you serve someone else in a humbling way?

When have you been overcome with grief and joy at the same time? When have you been deeply grieving a loss, but felt joy as well? From where did the joy come?

your closet and shared items with those who don't have a change of clothes. Donate the clothes and shoes that are in good shape to a local shelter. Maybe you (individually) need to apologize to someone, which can be a very humbling experience as well as good for the spirit.

In the Rear View

In the midst of Mary's deep grief at what she could see coming, she also demonstrated joy, a joy that exceeded a passing happiness. There is joy in the midst of grief. It is not easily explained and often can only be seen through symbolic acts such as Mary's.

There seems to have been an importance in understanding that the Messiah must die and in lavishing him with expensive perfume, while at the same time continuing to care for the poor of the world. As a group, identify different kinds of poverty (i.e. monetary, spiritual, emotional, social, etc.). Then talk together about ways of ministering to people who are living in various kinds of poverty.

Day 1:

In the Gospel of John, Jesus' raising of Lazarus caused the political and religious leaders to begin their plot against Jesus. In other Gospels, the catalyst was Jesus referring to himself as the "son of God" or simply becoming too popular. Why do you think John gave this particular moment so much significance in Jesus' journey to the cross? Journal your thoughts in the space below.

Day 2:

Gather old newspapers, magazines, tape or a glue stick, markers, and a piece of paper. Scan the magazines and papers for images that represent times when you have been filled with joy in the midst of grief. Cut them out and create a collage. An alternative would be to draw a picture or write scriptures or other words on your sheet of paper. Allow yourself the time and space to be creative. Once you have completed your collage, look at it and reflect on these sacred moments.

Day 3:

Find a scented candle that you enjoy smelling or spray some perfume in the space where you will pray. Sit quietly and breathe deeply, inhaling the fragrance. Imagine you are anointing the feet of Jesus and gently wiping his feet. What does Jesus say to you? What questions do you ask? Have a conversation with the Christ in your imagination. Once you have completed the conversation, write about your experience or make a list of things you heard Christ say to you.

Day 4:

Imagine that you are one of the other people present at the dinner. How do you react when Mary dares to join the gathering? How do you feel about what she does? What do you tell other people about it later? Record your answers below.

Day 5:

In many ways, the scripture for this lesson provides examples of two ways of being in the world. We can be like Mary, who lavished Jesus with love regardless of the cost. Or we can be like Judas, who held on to all he could, judging Mary who didn't. In truth, we each have some Mary and some Judas in us. Make a grid (like a pros/cons list) in the space below. List the ways you are like Mary and the ways you are like Judas. Be specific. Write examples of things you do that fall into each category. Reflect on your list. How balanced is it? In what ways would you prefer this list to be different? Note how you can make those changes.

Day 6:

Write using this prompt, "Six days before the Passover Jesus came to Bethany, the home of Lazarus, whom he had raised from the dead…" Do not edit what you have written; just continue to write. If you get stuck and feel like nothing is coming to you, go back to the prompt and write it again and again until something else comes to your mind. After approximately five minutes, read aloud what you have written. Reflect on surprises or things you learned about the passage from this experience.

Day 7:

What does joy mean to you? How do you experience joy? Make a list of the things that cause you to feel joyful. Identify ways of introducing more joy into your life.

Joy in the Work of the Gospel

Scripture for lesson:
Philippians 1:1-26

Written by Tiffany Hall McClung

While a seminary student, I worked as a youth minister for a medium-sized congregation in a Memphis suburb. The youth with whom I worked were from upper-middle class families and wanted for very little. Their idea of a summer youth trip was to cruise around the Gulf of Mexico for a weekend.

After accompanying them on a couple of these summer trips, I met with their parents and announced that rather than continuing the tradition of taking a cruise, I was going to Mexico to build houses for folks who had none and I hoped they would let me take their children with me. There were a lot of questions! There was a good deal of anxiety about safety. In the end, though, it was decided the summer trip would be in the context of mission. The most anxious parents decided to come with us to Mexico.

That trip changed all of our lives. It was hard work, probably the hardest I've ever worked, physically speaking. It was sad at times, especially when we arrived in the Mexican neighborhood and it hit us how these children of God had been living. But, mostly, it was filled with joy. By the end of the week, we had built six cinderblock homes that were about as big as one bedroom in our own houses back in the states. The families living in those new homes were thrilled to own them and reacted as if we had given them a palace.

We hoped, as we left, that we had changed the lives of those families for whom we had built houses. We knew without a doubt that they had changed ours. The gospel of Jesus Christ called us to Mexico to help others. His story is the one that spoke beyond language barriers. We had heard his story all our lives, but we were finally living it out in a tangible way. Doing this work brought a sense of joy we had never previously experienced.

How do you live out the gospel of Jesus Christ? What have you experienced as a result of those actions?

Who has made a difference in your past? How do you maintain contact with that person or group?

Paul specifies that every time he thinks of the congregation at Philippi he thanks God for them and prays for them. When has someone said something similar to you? When have you made such a comment to another person? How does it feel to be on the receiving end? on the giving end? What does it mean to stop and thank God for someone every time that person crosses your mind?

Prep for the Journey

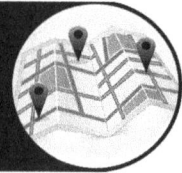

Read Philippians 1:1-5.

To all the saints in Christ Jesus who are in Philippi, with the bishops and deacons: ² Grace to you and peace from God our Father and the Lord Jesus Christ. ³ I thank my God every time I remember you, ⁴ constantly praying with joy in every one of my prayers for all of you, ⁵ because of your sharing in the gospel from the first day until now.

Eugene Peterson, in his introduction to the Book of Philippians in *The Message*, says that this is Paul's "happiest letter." From the very beginning, Paul's joy is evident even though it is clear that his circumstances are not joyful in the least. We know from many of the epistles in the New Testament that Paul's ministry was one on the move. The longest he stayed with any one congregation was a little more than two years. But, once he moved on to the next congregation, he did not forget the previous ones, maintaining his pastoral ministry through letters. Scholars presume that he wrote letters to his congregations with the understanding that they would be read aloud to the entire group.

The letter to the church in Philippi was written to inform, thank, and inspire the congregation. "It opens a window upon a relationship between the writer and the readers, a relationship which, by means of the letter, is remembered, enjoyed, nourished, and informed" (Craddock 2).

This particular letter was written while Paul was in prison awaiting trial, so Paul truly would not have known what the outcome of the situation would be. Some scholars say that according to custom at the time, Paul would have been under a sort of house arrest where he was constantly guarded—possibly even chained to a guard—but had to pay for his own housing, food, supplies, etc.

This information is important because it meant that Paul relied on his friends for monetary support while he awaited the Roman government's decision about his fate. He had been waiting for years when he wrote this letter, yet still he was filled with joy. His joy came from knowing that the work of the gospel was on-going—whether he lived or died, remained a prisoner or was set free. The work of the gospel would continue through people like those at Philippi.

On the Road

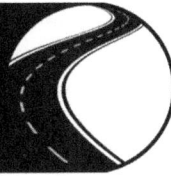

Read Philippians 1:6-11.

I am confident of this, that the one who began a good work among you will bring it to completion by the day of Jesus Christ. [7] *It is right for me to think this way about all of you, because you hold me in your heart, for all of you share in God's grace with me, both in my imprisonment and in the defense and confirmation of the gospel.* [8] *For God is my witness, how I long for all of you with the compassion of Christ Jesus.* [9] *And this is my prayer, that your love may overflow more and more with knowledge and full insight* [10] *to help you to determine what is best, so that in the day of Christ you may be pure and blameless,* [11] *having produced the harvest of righteousness that comes through Jesus Christ for the glory and praise of God.*

After addressing the past in earlier verses, Paul turned his attention to the present. Verses 3-11 make up what has come to be called "the Pauline Thanksgiving." Most of his letters begin this way as he shares with his congregation that for which he is thankful in and through them.

He continued to share his gratitude for the people of the Philippian church in that they not only had taken to heart the work of the gospel, but that they were living it out by sharing God's grace with him as he endured imprisonment. It is clear that they were among his strongest supporters, both spiritually and financially.

As Paul has thanked them for answering God's call in the past when he was with them physically, he also thanked them for the ways in which they were ministering to him in the present. Paul did not leave it there, though. Before he concluded his thanksgiving, he addressed the future as well. He shared with them his specific prayers for insight and blamelessness. He spoke about the coming of the Christ as "the day of Christ" and encouraged them to remain pure as they waited for that coming day. The bottom line is that God began the work of the gospel and Paul was assuring them that God would complete that work through them.

Scenic Route

Read Philippians 1:12-26.

I want you to know, beloved, that what has happened to me has actually helped to spread the gospel, [13] *so that it has become known*

Imagine you are writing a letter to your own faith community. What would your thanksgiving say? For what are you thankful about the past? the present? What do you hope for your faith community in the future?

Paul saw Christ at work in the imperial guard; where do you see Christ at work in those who feel like they imprison you? Where is Christ at work in those who seem phony to you or seem to be preaching for selfish reasons?

throughout the whole imperial guard and to everyone else that my imprisonment is for Christ; [14] and most of the brothers and sisters, having been made confident in the Lord by my imprisonment, dare to speak the word with greater boldness and without fear. [15] Some proclaim Christ from envy and rivalry, but others from goodwill. [16] These proclaim Christ out of love, knowing that I have been put here for the defense of the gospel; [17] the others proclaim Christ out of selfish ambition, not sincerely but intending to increase my suffering in my imprisonment. [18] What does it matter? Just this, that Christ is proclaimed in every way, whether out of false motives or true; and in that I rejoice. Yes, and I will continue to rejoice, [19] for I know that through your prayers and the help of the Spirit of Jesus Christ this will turn out for my deliverance. [20] It is my eager expectation and hope that I will not be put to shame in any way, but that by my speaking with all boldness, Christ will be exalted now as always in my body, whether by life or by death. [21] For to me, living is Christ and dying is gain. [22] If I am to live in the flesh, that means fruitful labor for me; and I do not know which I prefer. [23] I am hard pressed between the two: my desire is to depart and be with Christ, for that is far better; [24] but to remain in the flesh is more necessary for you. [25] Since I am convinced of this, I know that I will remain and continue with all of you for your progress and joy in faith, [26] so that I may share abundantly in your boasting in Christ Jesus when I come to you again.

Paul did not fill this letter with complaints about his imprisonment and long wait for a trial. Instead of complaining or despairing, Paul rejoiced at the work of the gospel happening in spite of, or sometimes because of, his predicament. What Paul really wanted the congregation to understand was that the work of the gospel would continue.

He wrote about the ways in which the gospel work had advanced because of his imprisonment. First, he mentioned the imperial guard. He didn't specify the ways in which the gospel had advanced through them, but he rejoiced in the mere fact that because these men had guarded him, they had heard the story of Jesus. Second, he described the newfound courage of other Christians to share the work of the gospel. It seems that Paul being in prison had empowered others to speak out and share the story of Jesus more boldly. And, third, he took time to mention something he seemed to find baffling, calling it unexpected. There were some who were preaching for their own gain rather than truly for Christ, yet Paul told of this joyfully. He explained that the motives of the preacher did not matter as long as the story of the gospel was being shared.

After sharing the ways in which the work of the gospel was continuing, Paul dove into the full range of emotions about his circumstances. He seemed to be torn about what he would prefer happen once his trial came. Should he live, he would joyfully continue to serve along with others like the congregation at Philippi. Should he die, he would joyfully enter into the eternal presence of Christ, his savior. Paul was not afraid to show his paradox of feelings to those in Philippi, which shows a certain amount of comfort with those who would hear his words. He was fully himself, questions and all, and completely joyful at being a part of the work of Christ regardless of what might come next.

Workers Ahead

Paul wrote a letter to the church in Philippi during a difficult time for himself. Rather than being filled with despair, he was filled with joy and hope. As a pastor, he attempted to pass along that joy and hope to those who would hear his letter.

We live in a world that sometimes feels like we are under house arrest! The news is bad and getting worse. Children continue to starve and be abused. Our political system has become a punch line. The earth grows more and more sick. Meanwhile, our own schedules have created a sort of prison for us while we lament not having time for the important matters of life.

Our world needs to hear the message of hope and joy found in the gospel of Christ, possibly more now than ever before. As Christians, it is our responsibility to share in the spreading of that message. As a group, talk about ways in which you and your faith community can share hope and joy in your community and beyond. Make specific plans and take action. Remember: Even if your efforts are not the best, God will still use them. Any attempt to spread the message of Christ will bear fruit.

In the Rear View

Paul cared a great deal about the congregation at Philippi; it is clear the feeling was mutual. As he found himself awaiting trial under house arrest, he wrote to this congregation to thank them and to encourage them to continue in the work of the gospel.

It is important to encourage and give thanks, even when it may feel difficult to do so. To whom do you need to offer encouragement to continue the work of the gospel?

When have you found yourself in the midst of a very difficult time? Paul was in prison, but saw the joy of what was going on around him. What similar experiences have you had?

How can you share the hope and joy in the work of the gospel in the midst of your own difficult times?

The word *rejoice* is used twice in quick succession in verses 18 and 19. Read through this section of the passage again. Why do you think Paul used that particular word? Why do you think he used it twice so close together? Reflect on what Paul may have wanted those hearing his letter to pick up from this choice.

Day 1:

What have been the positive life-changing moments in your life? How did you express joy for those times? Write a prayer thanking God for bringing such moments into your life.

Day 2:

Make a list of people for whom you are thankful. Paul said in his letter that every time he thought of the Philippians, he thanked God for them. Who are the Philippians in your life? Thank God for them.

Day 3:

Imagine yourself as the person who read aloud the letter from Paul to the Philippians. Write about the experience. Decide if you are writing before or after you have read the letter to the congregation. What are your thoughts? How are you feeling? How does the congregation react? What kinds of things do they say after hearing the letter? Be as specific as you can while imagining yourself in the situation.

Day 4:

Reflect on the scripture passage used with this lesson. What questions do you still have? In what ways do you feel the joy and hope Paul conveyed? In what ways are you still missing the joy and hope? Journal your responses.

Day 5:

If possible in your context, visit someone in prison. Such a visit may take some planning, and you will have to check with the local prison/jail to see what requirements are involved, but this could be a very powerful experience for you. If visiting is not an option, explore ways to write a letter to a prisoner. There may be someone connected with your congregation who is in prison. Get the person's address and send a letter of encouragement filled with joy and hope.

Day 6:

Write down the ways in which you see the advancement of the gospel in your life and in the lives of those around you. Look for the joy in those advancements. Share this joy and hope with others. Doing so could be as simple as injecting a note of hope into a conversation. Write a letter to someone who needs to know the ways God has used him or her in your life. There are millions of ways to inject hope and joy into the lives of those around you. Ask God to give you ideas, and then have the courage to act on those ideas.

Day 7:

Read Philippians 1:1-26, possibly in a version different from the one you normally use. Breathe deeply and take in every word as you read the passage. Write down images, words, or phrases that jump out at you. Rest as you know that in God there is great joy.

Works Cited:

Craddock, Fred. "Salutation: Paul Greets the Church and Its Leaders Philippians 1:1-2" *Philippians: Interpretation: A Bible Commentary for Teaching and Preaching.* Louisville: John Knox, 1985. 1-30. Print.